New edition

# Pronunciation

## Study Book

Jonathan Smith and Annette Margolis

**ISLC**
International Study
and Language Centre

**University of Reading**

*Garnet*
EDUCATION

# Credits

**Published by**

Garnet Publishing Ltd
8 Southern Court
South Street
Reading RG1 4QS, UK

This edition first published 2012

ISBN: 978 1 90861 435 3

British Cataloguing-in-Publication Data
A catalogue record for this book is available from the British Library.

**Production**

| | |
|---|---|
| Project manager: | Kayleigh Buller |
| Project consultant: | Fiona McGarry |
| Editorial team: | Kayleigh Buller, Fiona McGarry |
| Art director: | Mike Hinks |
| Design and layout: | Simon Ellway, Ian Lansley, Maddy Lane |
| Photography: | Mike Hinks |

Every effort has been made to trace the copyright holders and we apologize in advance for any unintentional omission. We will be happy to insert the appropriate acknowledgements in any subsequent editions.

**Printed and bound** in Lebanon by International Press: interpress@int-press.com

# Contents

# Book map

| | Topics | Objectives |
|---|---|---|
| **1** | ■ Vowel sounds: /æ/, /e/, /ɪ/, /ɒː/, /ɜː/, /iː/<br>■ Syllables and word stress<br>■ Weak forms in function words | ■ Learn which phonemic symbols represent certain vowel sounds<br>■ Practise recognizing and producing these vowel sounds<br>■ Learn about the concepts of the syllable and word stress<br>■ Practise producing words with the correct word stress;<br>■ Practise recognizing weak forms of function words when listening |
| **2** | ■ Vowel sounds: /ɒ/, /ʌ/, /ə/, /ʊ/, /ɔː/, /uː/<br>■ Unstressed syllables and word stress patterns | ■ Learn which phonemic symbols represent the other vowel sounds<br>■ Practise recognizing and producing these vowel sounds<br>■ Learn more about which syllable is stressed in some types of word |
| **3** | ■ Voiced and unvoiced consonants<br>■ Consonant sounds: /θ/, /ð/, /t/, /s/<br>■ Sentence stress | ■ Learn about the pronunciation of voiced and unvoiced consonants<br>■ Practise recognizing and producing these sounds<br>■ Learn to identify stressed words in sentences<br>■ Practise using sentence stress to highlight important information |
| **4** | ■ Consonant sounds: /ʒ/, /v/, /j/, /ʃ/, /tʃ/, /dʒ/<br>■ Word stress on two-syllable words | ■ Learn phonemic symbols representing consonant sounds<br>■ Practise recognizing and producing these consonant sounds<br>■ Learn where to place the stress in words with two syllables |
| **5** | ■ Diphthongs: /aɪ/, /əʊ/, /eɪ/<br>■ Sounds in connected speech: linking, insertion | ■ Learn which phonemic symbols represent certain diphthongs<br>■ Practise recognizing and producing diphthongs<br>■ Learn how the pronunciation of words is affected by their context in connected speech |
| **6** | ■ Consonant clusters: at the beginning and in the middle of words<br>■ Sounds in connected speech: disappearing sounds, contractions<br>■ Tone units | ■ Learn how to pronounce groups of consonants (consonant clusters) at the beginning and in the middle of words<br>■ Learn how to divide up connected speech into tone units |

| | Topics | Objectives |
|---|---|---|
| **7** | ■ Diphthongs: /aʊ/, /eə/, /ɪə/, /ɔɪ/<br>■ Sentence stress and tone units | ■ Learn which phonemic symbols represent other diphthongs<br>■ Practise recognizing and producing these diphthongs<br>■ Have more practice identifying sentence stress and tone units |
| **8** | ■ Consonant clusters: at the end of words and across two words<br>■ Intonation | ■ Learn how to pronounce consonant clusters at the end of words and across two words<br>■ Learn how intonation is used to organize and emphasize information |

# i Introduction

## Aims of the course:

The purpose of this book is to help you to improve the accuracy of your **pronunciation**, develop your listening **microskills**, learn the **phonemic alphabet**, build your understanding of sound/spelling relationships, recognize and remember words and phrases that commonly occur in academic contexts.

## Accuracy of pronunciation

Accurate pronunciation is important if you want people to understand you clearly. Frequent pronunciation errors may put a strain on the listener, and may also lead to breakdowns in communication. While you do not have to speak with a perfect English accent, your aim must be at least for your pronunciation to be good enough for the listener to understand you with ease. The main technique you can use to achieve this is to listen and repeat patterns of pronunciation, but learning the phonemic alphabet and developing a sensitive ear will also help you.

## Learning the phonemic alphabet

The phonemic alphabet is a system for showing the pronunciation of words in English, and is shown on page 9 of this book. At first glance, the phonemic alphabet looks like another language that you have to learn. However, about half of the 44 phonetic symbols that you are expected to know are pronounced in the same way as they are written. We have focused on:

- those symbols which may be unfamiliar, and so may be difficult to learn
- those sounds which may be difficult to pronounce for certain learners

We believe that learning the phonemic alphabet will help you to develop more accurate pronunciation and improve your listening skills. In addition, if you know the phonemic alphabet you can:

- understand the correct pronunciation when looking up a word in a dictionary
- note down the correct pronunciation in your vocabulary notebook

So, knowing the phonemic alphabet is another important aspect of recording and learning vocabulary.

## Listening microskills

In listening classes, you will have had practice understanding meaning that is built up over a sentence or several sentences, but you may have had difficulty with comprehension at a lower level. Listening microskills are the skills you need to understand meaning at the level of a word or small group of words.

Students frequently remark that there are many words that they know in their written form, but fail to recognize when listening. There may be several reasons for this; for example, words may not be pronounced in the way you expect them to be, or it may be difficult to hear where one word ends and another begins. Many activities in this book will help you to deal with such problems.

## Sound/spelling relationships

Another difficulty faced by students is that there does not seem to be a relationship between the way words are spelt in English and the way they are pronounced. This creates problems, not just for accurate pronunciation, but also for correct spelling. In fact, while there are exceptions (and many of these exceptions seem to relate to the most common words in English), there are a lot of useful **sound/spelling patterns**. If you can ensure that you are familiar with these patterns, you can then focus on learning the exceptions, which are the words that create the most problems.

## Academic vocabulary

The examples and exercises in these materials are focused on words from:
- the **General Service List** (GSL): the 2,000 most frequently used words in English
- the **Academic Word List** (AWL): a list of 570 word families that are most commonly used in academic contexts

All the words in the AWL will be useful to you, but some of the words in the GSL are either words you may know already (e.g., *you, from, hand*) or words that are not commonly or widely used in academic contexts (e.g., *handkerchief, niece, jealous*). In general, words like these have not been used in the examples and exercises.

In addition, a number of extracts from academic lectures have been used to provide practice in listening for features of pronunciation.

A lot of care has been taken, therefore, to ensure that the vocabulary focused on in this book is relevant to both academic study and your needs. Many words will be those you 'half know', so the materials should reinforce your understanding. Other words may be quite new to you.

## Structure of the course

There is a range of different exercises that require you to work in different ways. For example, you may need to:
- listen and repeat words or sentences
- stop the recording and read an explanation
- stop the recording, write words in spaces in sentences, then listen to check your answers
- stop the recording, fill in a table or choose the correct answer, then listen to check your answers

If you just play the recording non-stop, listening and reading at the same time, you will not improve your pronunciation or listening skills. You will have to stop the recording to read, think, write and check answers, and you will have to replay short sections you have difficulty with.
- **Pronunciation notes**
  Each unit has at least one *Pronunciation note*. These notes explain different rules relating to the content in that unit, for example, the pronunciation of consonant clusters.
- **Study tips**
  These are included for ease of reference when you are revising what you have studied. They either summarize the outcome of a series or activities or are a summary of other information contained in the unit.

## Listening material

This is available on CD and is indicated by the play icon ▶. The full transcripts for the audio material are available at the back of the book, starting on page 77.

### Recording your own voice
When you are asked to listen and repeat words, phrases or sentences, it can also be very useful to record your own voice and then play it back. This will enable you to compare your own pronunciation with the recording, and hear any differences or problems clearly. You will not need to record your voice for every exercise, but try to do this when you know you have a problem with certain aspects of pronunciation.

If you are unsure whether your pronunciation on an exercise is accurate enough, and you are working with a teacher, ask him or her to listen to your recording. He or she will be able to assess your pronunciation more objectively.

## Additional materials

**Glossary:** Words or phrases in **bold** (or **bold** and <u>underlined</u> in the task introductions) in the text are explained in the Glossary on page 75.

**Answer key:** Answers for all the exercises are provided.

**Transcripts:** Starting on page 77, you will find the transcripts of all the audio material. Your teacher will sometimes give you the opportunity to listen to the recordings and follow the transcript at the same time, once you have completed the main listening tasks.

# Phonemic alphabet

## Consonants

| /p/ | /t/ | /k/ | /s/ | /ʃ/ | /tʃ/ | /f/ | /θ/ |
|-----|-----|-----|-----|-----|------|-----|-----|
| post | take | keep | snow | shoe | choice | leaf | thin |
| /b/ | /d/ | /g/ | /z/ | /ʒ/ | /dʒ/ | /v/ | /ð/ |
| book | doctor | goal | zero | measure | jump | leave | the |
| /h/ | /m/ | /n/ | /ŋ/ | /l/ | /r/ | /w/ | /j/ |
| hotel | meet | nine | bring | late | red | well | yes |

## Vowels

| /æ/ | /e/ | /ɪ/ | /ɒ/ | /ʌ/ | /ə/ |
|-----|-----|-----|-----|-----|-----|
| plan | end | big | job | sum | the |
| /ʊ/ | /ɑː/ | /ɜː/ | /ɪː/ | /ɔː/ | /uː/ |
| good | car | her | fee | law | too |

## Diphthongs

| /aɪ/ | /aʊ/ | /əʊ/ | /eɪ/ | /eə/ | /ɪə/ | /ɔɪ/ | /ʊə/ |
|------|------|------|------|------|------|------|------|
| why | now | go | day | care | dear | enjoy | pure |

**Notes:**

1.  The sound /ə/ is very common in unstressed **syllables** in English. In this sentence it occurs seven times: *Poverty is at the centre of the problem.*

2.  The sound /ʊə/ is relatively uncommon in English.

3.  Many vowel or diphthong sounds can be spelt in different ways, e.g., /ɜː/ in *her*, *'turn*, *heard*, *word*, and many similar spellings can be pronounced in different ways, e.g., *head* /hed/, *heat* /hiːt/, *heart* /hɑːt/, *heard* /hɜːd/.

# 1 Vowel sounds 1, word stress and weak forms

In this unit you will:

- learn which **phonemic symbols** represent certain vowel sounds
- practise recognizing and producing these vowel sounds
- learn about the concepts of the syllable and **word stress**
- practise producing words with the correct word stress
- practise recognizing **weak forms** of **function words** when listening

There are 12 vowel sounds in English. In this unit, you will focus on the six sounds shaded in the table. You will also look at how vowels are used in syllables and are affected by word stress patterns.

| /æ/ | /e/ | /ɪ/ | /ɒ/ | /ʌ/ | /ə/ |
|------|------|------|------|------|------|
| pl<u>a</u>n | <u>e</u>nd | b<u>i</u>g | j<u>o</u>b | s<u>u</u>m | th<u>e</u> |
| /ʊ/ | /ɑ:/ | /ɜ:/ | /i:/ | /ɔ:/ | /u:/ |
| g<u>oo</u>d | c<u>a</u>r | h<u>er</u> | f<u>ee</u> | l<u>aw</u> | t<u>oo</u> |

## Task 1    Vowel sounds

1.1    ▶ **CD1: 1 Listen to the difference in the pronunciation of these pairs of words. In each of them the vowel sound is different.**

1. /ɪ/       /i:/
   fit       feet
   dip       deep
   hit       heat

2. /æ/       /e/
   mass      mess
   band      bend
   had       head

3. /æ/       /ɑ:/
   hat       heart
   match     march
   pack      park

4.  /e/          /ɜː/

ten          turn

head         heard

went         weren't

**Listen again and repeat the words.**

1.2    ▶ **CD1: 2 You will hear some of the words from Ex 1.1. Listen and circle the phonemic transcription that matches the pronunciation of the word you hear.**

1.  /hed/          (/hɜːd/)                6.  /went/        /wɜːnt/

2.  /pæk/          /pɑːk/                  7.  /dɪp/         /diːp/

3.  /ten/          /tɜːn/                  8.  /hæd/         /hed/

4.  /mæs/          /mes/                   9.  /hæt/         /hɑːt/

5.  /hɪt/          /hiːt/                  10. /bænd/        /bend/

**Note:** You can check all your answers at the back of the book on pages 102–112.

1.3    ▶ **CD1: 3 Listen to six more words and do activities a and b.**

a.  Listen and circle the phonemic transcription that matches the pronunciation of the word you hear.

1.  /sɪt/          _____          /siːt/          _____

2.  /mæt/          _____          /met/           _____

3.  /hɜːt/         _____          /hɑːt/          _____

4.  /fɑː/          _____          /fɜː/           _____

5.  /lɪv/          _____          /liːv/          _____

6.  /sæd/          _____          /sed/           _____

b.  Write the words, with the correct spelling, in the spaces next to the phonemic transcriptions.

### Study tip

Learners' dictionaries include phonemic transcriptions of all headwords. Use these to check the pronunciation of vocabulary you are uncertain about. It is also useful to remind yourself of the pronunciation of new words by transcribing them in your own notebook.

## Task 2 — Syllables

For pronunciation purposes, words can be divided into syllables. A syllable contains only one vowel sound, which may be preceded or followed by consonants. Remember that some consonants can also be pronounced as vowels; for example, *heavy* is a two-syllable word, because the ~y is pronounced as a vowel.

**2.1** ▶ **CD1: 4 Listen to these examples of one, two, three or more syllable words.**

**1.** one-syllable words

| aid | quote | source | fee |
|-----|-------|--------|-----|

**2.** two-syllable words

| cred•it | ac•cept | heav•y | e•quate |
|---------|---------|--------|---------|

**3.** three or more syllable words.

| pol•i•cy | sim•i•lar | en•vi•ron•ment | i•den•ti•fy | in•di•vid•ual |
|----------|-----------|----------------|-------------|---------------|

**2.2** ▶ **CD1: 5 Listen to these words and decide how many syllables there are in each of them.**

| | Syllables | | | Syllables |
|---|---|---|---|---|
| **1.** specific | _____ | | **6.** consequent | _____ |
| **2.** alter | _____ | | **7.** framework | _____ |
| **3.** resource | _____ | | **8.** significant | _____ |
| **4.** preliminary | _____ | | **9.** adapt | _____ |
| **5.** available | _____ | | **10.** differentiate | _____ |

> ➤ Pronunciation note ◄

There is some variation in the way people pronounce words and whether they 'drop' syllables in some multi-syllable words. For example, some people pronounce *preliminary* with four syllables /prɪˈlɪmɪnrɪ/, while other people pronounce it with five syllables /prɪˈlɪmɪnərɪ/.

## Task 3 — Word stress patterns

In words of more than one syllable, one syllable is emphasized more than others; it has a stronger sound than other syllables and is known as a *stressed* syllable. If you pronounce a word with the main stress on the wrong syllable, you will sometimes be misunderstood.

**Study tip**

In a dictionary, the stressed syllable of a word or phrase is indicated by an apostrophe (ʹ) – this is inserted before the stressed syllable.

**3.1**    ▶ **CD1: 6 Listen for the stressed syllable in these words.**
The stressed syllable is marked with (').

| | | | | |
|---|---|---|---|---|
| 'pol•i•cy | 'sim•i•lar | en•'vi•ron•ment | i•'den•ti•fy | in•di•'vid•ual |
| as•'sume | 'ma•jor | o•ver•'seas | op•e•'ra•tion | re•in•'force |

**3.2**    ▶ **CD1: 7 Listen again to the words from Ex 2.2. Mark the stressed syllables as shown in the example.**

**Example: 1.** spe'cific

**3.3**    ▶ **CD1: 8 Listen to the following sentences and mark the stressed syllable on the underlined words. The first one has been done for you.**

1. The pro'tection of children is the main 'purpose of this legislation.
2. The samples were analyzed in the lab.
3. Chemical analysis of the rock provided surprising results.
4. The aim of the study was to identify the factors contributing to domestic violence.
5. Periodicals are kept in an area on the ground floor.
6. The administration of these drugs needs to be closely monitored.
7. In percentage terms, this is not a significant increase.
8. This is the standard procedure for limiting the spread of the disease.

| Task 4 | Strong and weak forms of function words |
|---|---|

**4.1**    ▶ **CD1: 9 Listen to these pairs of sentences. What is the difference in the pronunciation of the underlined words in each pair? How can you explain this difference?**

1. a.  Interest rates are rising.
   b.  No, that's not true. We are doing something about it.
2. a.  Would you like some tea?
   b.  Most scientists are convinced about global warming, but some are not.
3. a.  Where's he coming from?
   b.  Results differed from one region to another.
4. a.  Is that your pen or mine?
   b.  Can I borrow your dictionary?

> ➤ Pronunciation note ◀

Ex 4.1 shows that the pronunciation of some **function words** is not always the same. Function words include conjunctions, pronouns, prepositions, articles, determiners and auxiliary verbs. They do not appear to have much meaning, but they have a grammatical function in the sentence.

Generally, a function word is unstressed and it very often uses the sound /ə/ instead of the full vowel. This reduced vowel sound is known as a **weak form**.

## ➤ Pronunciation note ◄

In the sentences in Ex 4.1, you will see that function words are <u>stressed</u> when they <u>add emphasis</u>, e.g., *No, that's not true. We <u>are</u> doing something about it.* This is also done to <u>indicate a contrast</u>, e.g., *Most scientists are convinced ..., but <u>some</u> are not.* You may also notice that function words at the end of sentences or questions have a strong form.

The following table contains some examples of these function words and their different pronunciations.

| | Stressed/Strong | Unstressed/Weak |
|---|---|---|
| but | /bʌt/ | /bət/ |
| than | /ðæn/ | /ðən/ |
| them | /ðem/ | /ðəm/ |
| you | /juː/ | /jə/ |
| at | /æt/ | /ət/ |
| for | /fɔː/ | /fə/ |
| the | /ðiː/ | /ðə/ |
| some | /sʌm/ | /səm/ |
| has | /hæz/ | /həz/, /əz/ |
| does | /dʌz/ | /dəz/ |
| can | /kæn/ | /kən/ |

**4.2** ▶ **CD1: 10 Listen to these sentences and write in the missing words, which are all weak forms of function words.**

1. One criticism levelled _____ the board was their lack _____ financial control.

2. This issue was discussed _____ some length during the conference.

3. These points should _____ been made more effectively.

4. How do we account _____ this change in behaviour?

5. This might do more harm _____ good.

6. This kind of restructuring is usually regarded by employees _____ a change _____ the worse.

7. This problem _____ easily be solved _____ minimal cost.

8. Trade sanctions will be imposed with effect _____ the 1st of December.

**4.3**  ▶ **CD1: 11 Study the following introduction from a lecture on globalization. Listen and write in the missing words. They are all weak forms of function words.**

Well, as Ros said, I'm going to talk about globalization today, which is one _____ the catchphrases, or buzzwords, if you like, _____ the late 20th _____ early 21st centuries. It's constantly in _____ news. It's used by politicians, by people in _____ media, by businesspeople, and when they're referring _____ globalization they talk about things like _____ way we _____ communicate almost instantaneously nowadays with people on the other side _____ _____ world by e-mail or by television. They're also talking about, _____ example, the way that _____ fall in share prices in one part _____ _____ world, _____ example, in the Far East, _____ have an immediate impact on the stock markets on the other side _____ _____ world, like in London or Frankfurt.

**4.4**  ▶ **CD1: 12 Listen to these phrases and repeat them. Can you identify and produce the weak forms of the function words?**

1. past and present figures
2. more or less fifty
3. they were selected at random
4. it was far from clear
5. the results of the trials

6. too good to be true
7. needless to say
8. it's gone from bad to worse
9. we'll have to wait and see
10. we had some problems

## Unit summary

In this unit, you have learnt six English vowel sounds: /ɪ/, /iː/, /e/, /ɜː/, /æ/, /ɑː/, and practised their pronunciation. You have also become more aware of syllables and word stress, and practised listening for weak forms of function words.

**1** **Say the words in the box aloud. Decide how many syllables there are in each word and write them in the correct spaces below.**

| globalization | century | constantly | politician |
|---|---|---|---|
| refer | media | financial | market |

a. two-syllable words: _____

b. three-syllable words: _____

c. four-syllable words: _____

d. five-syllable words: _____

**2** ▶ **CD1: 13 Now listen to the words from Ex 1 and mark the stressed syllable in each word.**

**3** **Which of the stressed syllables you marked in Ex 2 have the following vowel sounds?**
**Note: Only six of the words contain these sounds.**

/ɪ/   /iː/   /e/   /ɜː/   /æ/   /ɑː/

**4** **Read the following sentences. Which words would usually be pronounced using a weak form?**
a. Globalization is one of the buzzwords of the 21st century.
b. It's constantly in the news and is often referred to by politicians and the media.
c. A fall in share prices in one part of the world can have an impact on the stock markets on the other side of the world.

**5** **Think about these questions.**
a. Why do you think learners confuse some of the vowel sounds you have practised in this unit?
b. Why is it useful to make a note of the stressed syllable when you learn a new multi-syllable word?
c. How can you check the correct stress and number of syllables in words that you learn in English?

For web resources relevant to this book, see:
**www.englishforacademicstudy.com**

This weblink will provide you with further practice in areas of pronunciation such as the sounds, stress and intonation patterns of English.

# 2 Vowel sounds 2, word stress patterns

In this unit you will:

- learn which phonemic symbols represent the other vowel sounds
- practise recognizing and producing these vowel sounds
- learn more about which syllable is stressed in some types of word

In Unit 1, you looked at six vowel sounds. In this unit, you will focus on the other six vowel sounds shaded in the table below. You will also practise using sounds in stressed and unstressed syllables and look more closely at common word stress patterns.

| /æ/ | /e/ | /ɪ/ | /ɒ/ | /ʌ/ | /ə/ |
|-----|-----|-----|-----|-----|-----|
| plan | end | big | job | sum | the |
| /ʊ/ | /ɑː/ | /ɜː/ | /ɪː/ | /ɔː/ | /uː/ |
| good | car | her | fee | law | too |

## Task 1 Vowel sounds

1.1 ► CD1: 14 **Listen to the difference in the pronunciation of these pairs of words. In each of them the vowel sound is different.**

1. /æ/ /ʌ/

   match  much
   lack   luck
   ankle  uncle

2. /ʊ/ /uː/

   pull   pool
   soot   suit
   full   fool

3. /ɒ/ /ɔː/

   spot   sport
   shot   short
   stock  stalk

4. /ɒ/          /ʊ/

lock          look

box           books

shock         shook

**Listen again and repeat the words.**

1.2     ▶ **CD1: 15 You will hear some of the words from Ex 1.1. Listen and circle the phonemic transcription that matches the pronunciation of the word you hear.**

1. (/læk/)          /lʌk/              6. /ænkəl/          /ʌnkəl/
2. /bɒks/           /bʊks/             7. /fʊl/            /fuːl/
3. /pʊl/            /puːl/             8. /lɒk/            /lʌk/
4. /spɒt/           /spɔːt/            9. /stɒk/           /stɔːk/
5. /mætʃ/           /mʌtʃ/             10. /ʃɒt/           /ʃɔːt/

1.3     ▶ **CD1: 16 Listen to six more words and do activities a and b.**

a.  Listen and circle the phonemic transcription that matches the pronunciation of the word you hear.

1. /fæn/     _____          /fʌn/      _____
2. /muːd/    _____          /mʌd/      _____
3. /kuːl/    _____          /kɔːl/     _____
4. /buːt/    _____          /bɔːt/     _____
5. /fʊt/     _____          /fuːd/     _____
6. /kʊd/     _____          /kɑːd/     _____

b.  Write the words, with the correct spelling, in the spaces next to the phonemic transcriptions.

| Task 2 | Unstressed syllables: /ə/ and /ɪ/ |

**Short /ə/**

The short /ə/ sound *only* appears in *unstressed* syllables. As can be seen from the examples given on the next page, there is no single written vowel form to represent /ə/. At the end of words, it may appear in written form as ~er, ~re, ~our, or ~or (as in *reader, meagre, favour,* and *actor*). **Note:** Many words ending with ~our in British English end with ~or in American English: *favour/favor, flavour/flavor, harbour/harbor,* etc.

**2.1** ▶ **CD1: 17 Listen to these examples.**

| | | | |
|---|---|---|---|
| appear /əˈpɪə/ | suggest /səˈdʒest/ | effort /ˈefət/ | colour /ˈkʌlə/ |

**2.2** **Study words 1–15 and do activities a–c.**

    **a.** Mark the stressed syllable with (ˈ).

    1.  comˈputer              9.  attempt

    2.  affect                 10.  distance

    3.  several               11.  accept

    4.  standard             12.  opposite

    5.  failure               13.  flavour

    6.  purpose             14.  compare

    7.  propose             15.  approach

    8.  author

    **b.** Write /ə/ above any syllables that include this sound.

    **c.** ▶ **CD1: 18** Listen and repeat the words.

**Short /ɪ/**

In unstressed syllables where the vowel letter is written as *e*, it is often pronounced as a short /ɪ/.

**2.3** ▶ **CD1: 19 Listen to these examples.**

| | |
|---|---|
| describe /dɪsˈkraɪb/ | prefer /prɪˈfɜː/ |

**2.4** **Study the words 1–8 and do activities a–c.**

    **a.** Mark the stressed syllable with (ˈ).

    1.  reˈduce              5.  beyond

    2.  invited               6.  extensive

    3.  decision            7.  research

    4.  demand            8.  interpret

    **b.** Write /ɪ/ above any syllables that include this sound.

    **c.** ▶ **CD1: 20** Listen and repeat the words.

Groups of nouns, adjectives and verbs with similar endings (or **suffixes**) often follow similar word stress patterns. In the groups of words below, the stress falls on the syllable before the ending (e.g.,~*sion*, ~*tion*, ~*graphy*, etc.)

3.1    ▶ **CD1: 21 Listen and repeat the following words, making sure you stress the syllables in the columns highlighted in the tables below.**

**Nouns ending in ~*sion* or ~*tion***

| | | | |
|---|---|---|---|
| version | | VER | sion |
| solution | so | LU | tion |
| occasion | oc | CA | sion |
| definition | defi | NI | tion |
| decision | de | CI | sion |
| position | po | SI | tion |

**Nouns ending in ~*graphy***

| | | | |
|---|---|---|---|
| geography | ge | OG | raphy |
| biography | bi | OG | raphy |
| photography | pho | TOG | raphy |

**Adjectives ending in ~*ic***

| | | | |
|---|---|---|---|
| electric | e | LEC | tric |
| economic | eco | NOM | ic |
| specific | spe | CIF | ic |

**Nouns ending in ~*ency* or ~*ancy***

| | | | |
|---|---|---|---|
| frequency | | FRE | quency |
| consultancy | con | SUL | tancy |
| consistency | con | SIS | tency |
| vacancy | | VA | cancy |
| efficiency | ef | FI | ciency |
| redundancy | re | DUN | dancy |

**Nouns ending in ~*ium***

| | | | |
|---|---|---|---|
| medium | | ME | dium |
| uranium | u | RAN | nium |
| consortium | con | SOR | tium |

### Adjectives ending in ~*ical*

| | | | |
|---|---|---|---|
| electrical | e | LEC | trical |
| political | po | LIT | ical |
| periodical | peri | OD | ical |

### Nouns ending in ~*ity*

| | | | |
|---|---|---|---|
| identity | i | DEN | tity |
| authority | au | THOR | ity |
| community | com | MU | nity |

### Adjectives ending in ~*tial* or ~*cial*

| | | | |
|---|---|---|---|
| essential | es | SEN | tial |
| financial | fi | NAN | cial |
| potential | po | TEN | tial |
| commercial | com | MER | cial |
| residential | resi | DEN | tial |
| artificial | arti | FI | cial |

### Verbs ending in ~*ify*

| | | | |
|---|---|---|---|
| modify | | MOD | ify |
| clarify | | CLAR | ify |
| identify | i | DEN | tify |

### Nouns ending in ~*logy*

| | | | |
|---|---|---|---|
| apology | a | POL | ogy |
| technology | tech | NOL | ogy |
| biology | bi | OL | ogy |

### Adjectives ending in ~*tional* or ~*sional*

| | | | |
|---|---|---|---|
| additional | ad | DI | tional |
| international | inter | NA | tional |
| optional | | OP | tional |

> **➤ Pronunciation note ◄**

In some words, the stressed syllable may change when the word is used as part of a compound noun. For example, *eco'nomic is* usually stressed on the third syllable, but in the phrase *'economic growth* the first syllable may be stressed instead.

**3.2** **Study the words below and do activities a and b.**

a. Mark the stressed syllable in each word, following the patterns in Ex 3.1.

1. academic
2. dimension
3. beneficial
4. similarity
5. majority
6. initial

7. demography
8. allergic
9. tradition
10. deficiency
11. conventional
12. justify

b. ▶ **CD1: 22** Listen to check your answers. Repeat the words to practise your pronunciation.

**3.3** **Study the sentences below. Use words from Ex 3.1 to complete the sentences.**

1. Most of the course modules are compulsory, but there are two _____ modules.

2. The committee has not yet taken a _____ whether or not to award funding for the project.

3. It is important to start with a _____ of the term 'sustainable development', as it clearly means different things to different people.

4. Although solar power provides a _____ answer to some of the world's energy needs, at the moment the technology is quite expensive.

5. Have we really found a _____ to the problem?

6. It is hoped that the development of _____ intelligence will mean that computers will be able to think in the way humans do.

7. There is a lot of confusion, so it is essential to _____ the situation.

8. The stadium was built by an international _____ of construction companies.

9. There is a _____ for a laboratory technician, so the post will be advertised next week.

10. James Watson's _____ of Margaret Thatcher was published last month.

11. The organization plans to publish a new _____, with three issues a year.

12. Would you like me to bring anything _____ to dinner next week?

13. We will need to _____ the design of the equipment after a number of weaknesses were discovered in the testing process.

14. Professor Jones is a leading _____ on 17ᵗʰ-century Italian literature.

15. The _____ areas of the new town will be located well away from the industrial and commercial zones.

▶ **CD1: 23 Listen to check your answers. Practise your pronunciation by playing the recording again and pausing to repeat the sentences.**

| Task 4 | Word families: Word stress and pronunciation |
| --- | --- |

**Word families** are groups of words that have the same basic form and similar meanings. By adding prefixes or suffixes, you can generate nouns, adjectives, adverbs and verbs from the basic form. Learning word families is a useful technique for extending your range of vocabulary.

**Word stress**
In many cases, the word stress pattern does not change from one form of the word to another.

4.1    ▶ **CD1: 24 Listen to the examples.**

| Verb | Noun | Adjective |
| --- | --- | --- |
| poss'ess | poss'ession | poss'essive |
| per'suade | per'suasion | per'suasive |
| ass'ess | ass'essment | ass'essed |

**However, in some cases the word stress may vary from one form to another.**

| 'analyze (v) | an'alysis (n) | ana'lytical (adj) |
| --- | --- | --- |

4.2    ▶ **CD1: 25 Listen and repeat these words. Mark the stressed syllable. The first one is done for you.**

| Verb | Noun | Adjective |
| --- | --- | --- |
| ap'ply | appli'cation | ap'plicable |
| activate | activity | active |
| inform | information | informative |
| – | probability | probable |
| socialize | society | social |
| experiment | experiment | experimental |
| equal | equality | equal |
| unite | union | united |
| transfer | transfer | transferable |

You may also notice differences in the vowel or consonant sounds. For example, in *social* /ˈsəʊʃl/ and *society* /səˈsaɪətiː/, the first vowel sound is different in each word.

Even when the word stress does not change, there may be differences in pronunciation of the basic form.

4.3 ▶ **CD1: 26 Listen to these examples.**

| | |
|---|---|
| occur (v) /əˈkɜː/ | occurrence (n) /əˈkʌrəns/ |
| assume (v) /əˈsjuːm/ | assumption (n) /əˈsʌmpʃən/ |

4.4 **Study the groups of sentences below and do activities a and b.**

**a.** Complete the gaps with a form of the underlined word in the first sentence.

1. We need to 'analyze the data.

   Statistical _____a'nalysis_____ of the data provided some unexpected results.

   You need good _____ana'lytical_____ skills for this kind of work.

2. The stomach pro'duces acids, which help to digest food.

   The new model should be in _____ in November.

   If the factory does not become more _____, it faces closure.

   The _____ was withdrawn from sale after a number of defects were identified.

3. Four alternative 'methods of payment are offered.

   She takes a very _____ approach to her work.

   They have been developing a new _____ for research in this area.

4. The president stated that eco'nomic development was the main priority.

   The chancellor is concerned that the _____ is overheating.

   She is studying _____ at Lancaster University.

5. Wages tend to be higher in the 'private sector.

   This law is intended to protect people's _____.

   The water services industry was _____ in the 1980s.

6. The heights of plants 'varied from 8 cm to 15 cm.

   A wide _____ of fruit is grown on the island.

   Regional _____ in the unemployment rate are significant.

   A number of _____, such as wind speed and direction, humidity and air pressure, need to be considered.

7.  Both approaches yielded 'similar results.

   There are many _____ between the two religions.

   The firefighters resorted to industrial action to settle the dispute. _____, railway workers are threatening to strike because of changes in working practices.

b.  Mark the stressed syllable in the words that you write in the gaps.

---

**> Pronunciation note <**

American English generally has similar word stress patterns to British English, but there are some notable cases where different syllables are stressed in American English. Example: 'laboratory (Am), lab'oratory (Br); 'controversy (Am), con'troversy (Br); 'advertisement (Am), ad'vertisement (Br).

**Study tip**

Experiment with different ways of marking word stress until you find the way that suits you best. You may find it helpful to underline the stressed syllable or draw a circle or box above the stressed vowel.

---

▶ **CD1: 27 Listen to the sentences and correct any that you got wrong.**

## Unit summary

In this unit, you have learnt six English vowel sounds: /ɒ/, /ʌ/, /ə/, /ʊ/, /ɔ:/, /u:/, and practised their pronunciation. You have also become more aware of weak forms and looked at different word stress patterns.

**1** ▶ **CD1: 28 Listen to the words in the box. Then match them to the phonemic transcriptions below.**

| | | | | | | | |
|---|---|---|---|---|---|---|---|
| other | ankle | pull | shot | uncle | pool | short | another |

a. /ənʌðə/ _____

b. /pu:l/ _____

c. /ʃɔːt/ _____

d. /pʊl/ _____

e. /ʌŋkəl/ _____

f. /æŋkəl/ _____

g. /ʌðə/ _____

h. /ʃɒt/ _____

**2** **Choose seven multi-syllable nouns that are connected with your field of study. If you like, you can include words that you have already studied in this unit. For each word, do the following:**

a. Write the word and mark the syllable that is stressed.

b. Check the pronunciation of the word in a learner's dictionary. Do you pronounce the unstressed syllable(s) using the sounds /ə/ or /ɪ/?

c. Does the word belong to a **word family**? Write as many other related words as you can think of, e.g., verb and adjective forms or other nouns with the same root.

For web resources relevant to this book, see:
**www.englishforacademicstudy.com**

This weblink will provide you with further practice in areas of pronunciation such as the sounds, stress and intonation patterns of English.

# 3

# Consonant sounds 1, sentence stress

In this unit you will:

- learn about the pronunciation of **voiced** and **unvoiced consonants**
- practise recognizing and producing these sounds
- learn to identify stressed words in sentences
- practise using **sentence stress** to highlight important information

In Units 1 and 2, you studied vowel sounds. You will now look at consonants, particularly consonants that English for Academic Purposes (EAP) students often find hard to pronounce. You will also look at how English speakers stress certain words in phrases and sentences.

## Task 1    Voiced and unvoiced consonants

When you pronounce a vowel, air passes freely through the mouth. When you pronounce a consonant, the air stream may be totally or partially obstructed (blocked) by the tongue, teeth or lips.

There are a number of pairs of consonants that are pronounced in the same way, except that one consonant is *unvoiced* and the other is *voiced*.

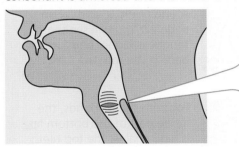

For **voiced** consonants /b/, /d/, /g/, etc., the vocal chords in your throat vibrate.

For **unvoiced** consonants /p/, /t/, /k/, etc., there is no vibration.

1.1    ▶ **CD1: 29 Listen and repeat these continuous consonant sounds and some words that contain them. What is the difference between them?**

/s/   snow, race

/z/   zero, raise

The position of your tongue, lips and mouth is more or less the same for each sound, but for the /z/ sound there is also a vibration of your vocal chords, so we say that /z/ is a *voiced* consonant. There is no vibration for the /s/ sound, so it is *unvoiced*.

In the table in Ex 1.2, each pair of consonants (/p/ and /b/, /t/ and /d/, etc.) is pronounced in the same way, except that one is voiced and the other is unvoiced.

**1.2** ▶ **CD1: 30 Listen and repeat each pair of words from the table. Can you hear the difference in pronunciation?**

| Unvoiced | | Voiced | |
|---|---|---|---|
| /p/ | pie | /b/ | buy |
| /t/ | town | /d/ | down |
| /k/ | coal | /g/ | goal |
| /s/ | sink | /z/ | zinc |
| /ʃ/ | mesh | /ʒ/ | measure |
| /tʃ/ | chunk | /dʒ/ | junk |
| /f/ | fast | /v/ | vast |
| /θ/ | breath | /ð/ | breathe |

/ʃ/ is unvoiced, e.g., me<u>sh</u>

/z/ is voiced, e.g., mea<u>s</u>ure

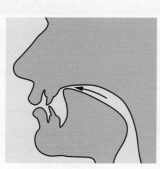

For both these sounds, the tongue is held close to the roof of the mouth. There is a narrow gap through which you force air. Compare these sounds with /s/ and /z/ on page 27. You will see the tongue is higher and further back in the mouth.

/f/ is unvoiced, e.g., <u>f</u>ast

/v/ is voiced, e.g., <u>v</u>ast

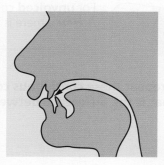

For both these sounds, the inside part of the bottom lip is held against the top teeth. Pressure is released as you bring the bottom lip away from the top teeth.

**Study tip**

You can check that you are producing voiced consonants correctly if you put your fingers on your throat as you say them. You should be able to feel your vocal chords vibrate.

**1.3** ▶ **CD1: 31 Listen to the following words and circle the one you hear.**

Each pair is pronounced in the same way except that one consonant is unvoiced and the other is voiced.

| | Unvoiced | Voiced | | Unvoiced | Voiced |
|---|---|---|---|---|---|
| **1.** | pill | (bill) | **5.** | try | dry |
| **2.** | paste | based | **6.** | white | wide |
| **3.** | simple | symbol | **7.** | card | guard |
| **4.** | tense | dense | **8.** | class | glass |

| 9. | ankle | angle | 14. | rich | ridge |
|---|---|---|---|---|---|
| 10. | sown | zone | 15. | batch | badge |
| 11. | price | prize | 16. | few | view |
| 12. | use (*n*) | use (*v*) | 17. | proof | prove |
| 13. | advice | advise | 18. | belief | believe |

▶ **CD1: 31 Then listen and repeat the words with the correct voiced or unvoiced consonant.**

> ➤ **Pronunciation note** ◄

It is not always easy to distinguish voiced and unvoiced consonants. This can be particularly difficult when they are at the ends of words where the voicing of some consonants may be reduced, e.g., *hard/heart*.

1.4 ▶ **CD1: 32 Listen and complete these sentences or phrases.**

1. a. a _____ situation _____
   b. a _____ material _V_

2. a. a _____ area _____
   b. as _____ as a sheet _____

3. a. at the _____ of the plant _____
   b. the _____ of change _____

4. a. Public _____ have improved. _____
   b. A cube has six _____. _____

5. a. difficult to _____ _____
   b. It's had good _____. _____

6. a. the _____ of the fire _____
   b. It changed the _____ of his life. _____

1.5 **Write *U* or *V* in the boxes provided to show if the missing word has an unvoiced or voiced consonant.**

1.6 ▶ **CD1: 32 Listen again and repeat the sentences or phrases, focusing on accurate pronunciation.**

## Task 2 /θ/, /t/ and /s/ <u>th</u>ink, <u>t</u>ime, <u>s</u>end

**2.1** ▶ **CD1: 33 Listen to the difference in pronunciation between these pairs of words.**

| /θ/ | /s/ |
|---|---|
| thing | sing |
| path | pass |
| worth | worse |
| mouth | mouse |
| youth | use |

| /θ/ | /t/ |
|---|---|
| thin | tin |
| thank | tank |
| thread | tread |
| both | boat |
| death | debt |

▶ **CD1: 33 Listen again and repeat the words.**

> ➤ **Pronunciation note** ◄

/θ/ is always written as *th* (*think*, *both*).

**2.2** ▶ **CD1: 34 You will hear some of the words from Ex 2.1. Circle the phonemic transcription that matches the pronunciation of the word you hear.**

| | | |
|---|---|---|
| 1. | /θɪn/ | /tɪn/ |
| 2. | /θæŋk/ | /tæŋk/ |
| 3. | /deθ/ | /det/ |
| 4. | /bəʊθ/ | /bəʊt/ |
| 5. | /wɜːθ/ | /wɜːs/ |
| 6. | /pɑːθ/ | /pɑːs/ |
| 7. | /maʊθ/ | /maʊs/ |
| 8. | /juːθ/ | /juːs/ |

**2.3**　　**Complete these sentences with words from Ex 2.1.**

1. The painting is supposed to be _____ £5 million.

2. The fuel is stored in a 30-litre _____.

3. Cancer is the leading cause of _____ among women.

4. A_____ layer of plastic is needed to provide waterproofing.

5. I couldn't follow the _____ of his argument.

6. The _____ is, no one likes to be criticized.

7. Tax increases are necessary to finance the national _____.

**2.4**　　▶　**CD1: 35 Listen to the correct answers and repeat the sentences.**

| Task 3 | /ð/ that |
|--------|----------|

/ð/ occurs as the first sound in a number of common function words.

**3.1**　　▶　**CD1: 36 Listen and repeat these words.**

| the | this | these | that | those | they |
|-----|------|-------|------|-------|------|
| their* | there* | theirs | than | then | though |

\* These words have the same pronunciation.

/ð/ also occurs at the end of some common words as /ðə/, spelt ~ther.

| weather** | whether** | gather | either | neither |
|-----------|-----------|--------|--------|---------|
| together | bother | rather | other | another |
| further | mother | father | brother | |

\*\* These words have the same pronunciation.

**3.2**　　▶　**CD1: 37 Listen to these sentences and phrases and repeat them.**

1. What's the weather like there?

2. Let's get together.

3. I'd rather not.

4. I wouldn't bother.

5. I don't like them.

6. I don't like them, either.

7. … further down the road …

8. … the other day …

## Task 4    /θ/ and /ð/ think, that

/θ/ is *unvoiced*, e.g., *thin*

/ð/ is *voiced*, e.g., *the*

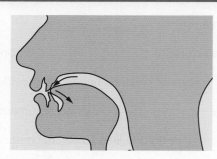

For both these sounds, the tip of the tongue is held against the back of the teeth. Pressure is released as you bring the tip of the tongue away from the teeth.

**4.1** ▶ **CD1: 38 Listen to these two words.**

thank    /θæŋk/

than    /ðæn/

To pronounce both /θ/ and /ð/, you put the tip of your tongue between your teeth, but /ð/ is also *voiced*. Can you hear how /ð/ has a heavier sound than /θ/?

**4.2** ▶ **CD1: 39 Listen to these phrases and write in the correct symbols above the words.**

           ð       θ

1. … another thing to consider is …

2. … in theory …

3. … the truth is that …

4. … the growth rate …

5. … a further theme …

6. … they thought that ….

7. … this method …

8. … beneath the surface …

9. … this therapy might be used to …

10. … youth culture …

▶ **CD1: 39 Now listen again and repeat the phrases.**

> ➤ Pronunciation note ◄

If you find the /θ/ sound difficult to pronounce, people should still understand from the context if you replace it with the /s/ sound or the /t/ sound.

| So, if you can't say … | try saying … |
| --- | --- |
| thank | sank, tank |
| thin | sin, tin |
| worth | worse |

Similarly, if you find the /ð/ sound difficult to pronounce, people should still understand from the context if you replace it with the /z/ sound or the /d/ sound.

| So, if you can't say … | try saying … |
|---|---|
| they | day |
| then | zen, den |
| breathe | breeze |

## Task 5 — Sentence stress

While word stress (or accent) is generally decided by language rules, sentence stress (or prominence) is decided by speaker choice. The speaker usually chooses to stress content words, which carry the information, and not structure or function words, such as auxiliary verbs, pronouns, prepositions and determiners, although this is not always the case.

**5.1** ▶ **CD1: 40 Listen to the paragraph. Notice which words are stressed.**

> So whose responsibility is it to ensure that children eat healthily? Well, clearly parents have a role, but while children are at school, it's difficult to keep track of what they are eating, so some would suggest that schools need to encourage healthy eating, and that this should be reflected in the menus they offer. Then there's the food industry. They've been criticized in the past for high levels of sugar, fat and salt in food and for not giving clear information on the levels of different ingredients in food. And finally there's the government. Should legislation be used to address this issue?

**5.2** ▶ **CD1: 41 Listen to these sentences in which the stress changes according to the meaning. Practise repeating them with the correct stress.**

1. You have to <u>hand in</u> the essay on Monday — … there's a strict <u>deadline</u>.

2. You have to hand in <u>the essay</u> on Monday — … not the <u>report</u>.

3. You have to hand in the essay on <u>Monday</u> — … not <u>Wednesday</u>.

**5.3** ▶ **CD1: 42 Listen to the beginnings of the sentences and choose the most suitable ending, according to the sentence stress.**

1. Well, we know how this happened, …

   ☐ … but do other people know?

   ☐ … but do we know why it happened?

2. Having looked at the effect of deforestation on the environment, …

   ☐ … we will now discuss greenhouse gases and the roles they play.

   ☐ … we will now consider its effect on the economy.

**3.** Most of our cotton is imported, …

☐ … but we produce about 500,000 tonnes a year.

☐ … but we are self-sufficient in wool.

**4.** The crime rate fell by 15 per cent last year, …

☐ … but this year it's risen.

☐ … but this year the figure is nearer to eight per cent.

**5.** The oil pump needs replacing, …

☐ … not the filter.

☐ … as it can't be repaired.

**5.4** ▶ **CD1: 43 Now listen to the complete sentences to check your answers.**
Can you hear how words are contrasted through stress in the different parts of each sentence?

**5.5** ▶ **CD1: 44 Read and listen to an extract from a lecture called *Introduction to British Agriculture*. Underline any stressed words that you hear.**

> As a backdrop to all of these activities, particularly after the Second World War, a lot of effort was put into research and development of agriculture in terms of plant breeding, breeding crops that were higher yielding, that were perhaps disease-resistant, and so on and so forth. Also, crops that might have better quality, better bread-making quality, higher gluten content, to make them doughy, higher protein content, and so on and so forth. Research, too, and this is again at one of the university farms, research into livestock production. Understanding how to better manage our livestock, again to make them produce more, certainly, but also to produce and influence the quality of the livestock products, whether that happens to be milk or cheese, come back to that in a moment, or indeed meat.

**5.6** ▶ **CD1: 44 Listen to the extract again and repeat it sentence by sentence. Why do you think the speaker chose to stress those words?**

**5.7** ▶ **CD1: 45 Read and listen to part of a lecture on globalization. Underline any stressed words that you hear.**

Now to get to the meat of the lecture, the basic purpose of this lecture is to give you some overview of the kind of contemporary academic and policy debate about globalization and particularly about a very specific, although rather general, debate itself, that is the debate on the effect of globalization on the role of the state. So, you see on the overhead the lecture's going to be kind of in two parts: the first will be looking at globalization, causes and consequences, and more particularly a kind of definition of the discussion of some of the competing conceptions of globalization, that is, you know, what people say it is, so that we can then discuss in some detail, hopefully, this question of how globalization's affecting the state.

**Study tip**

In rapid speech, good listeners unconsciously listen for the stressed words rather than trying to hear every word or syllable. Try to identify the words that your lecturers put most stress on, as this will help you follow the lecture and pick out key points.

**5.8** ▶ **CD1: 45 Listen to the extract again and repeat it sentence by sentence. Why do you think the speaker chose to stress those words?**

## Unit summary

In this unit, you have learnt about voiced and unvoiced consonant sounds, practised distinguishing between commonly confused sounds and focused on pronouncing the sounds /θ/ and /ð/. You have also become more aware of sentence stress and how it is used to highlight information.

**1 Study the words in the box and say them aloud. Then do activities a and b.**

a. Which words have a similar pronunciation and could be confused?

| | | | | | |
|---|---|---|---|---|---|
| lose | proof | surge | three | very | seem |
| free | theme | loose | ferry | prove | search |

b. Can you think of any other English words that are easily confused with each other?

**2 Practise saying the sentences by stressing the underlined words.**

a. You can take notes <u>during</u> the lecture or <u>after</u> it.

You <u>can</u> take notes during the lecture, but you don't <u>have</u> to.

<u>You</u> can take notes during the lecture, but <u>I'm</u> not going to!

b. <u>Exports</u> rose by three per cent last year, but <u>imports</u> fell.

Exports <u>rose</u> by three per cent last year, after years of <u>decline</u>.

Exports rose by <u>three</u> per cent last year, not the <u>eight</u> per cent reported in the media.

**3 In each sentence, underline two words that you would expect to be stressed to contrast information. Practise saying the sentences with these words stressed.**

a. Some species of shark attack people, but most are harmless.
b. There used to be a Chemistry department, but it closed in 2006.
c. The aid provided to the victims was too little, too late.
d. Many banks stopped lending, when the government wanted them to lend more.

▶ **CD1: 46 Listen and compare your ideas with the recording.**

**4 Think about what you have studied in this unit and answer the questions below.**

a. Which exercises did you find most challenging?
b. Which consonant sounds do you find confusing or find difficult to pronounce?
c. How is it helpful to study the phonemic symbols for different sounds?
d. Why is it helpful to be more aware of stressed words in a sentence?

For web resources relevant to this book, see:
**www.englishforacademicstudy.com**

This weblink will provide you with further practice in areas of pronunciation such as the sounds, stress and intonation patterns of English.

# Consonant sounds 2, word stress on two-syllable words

4

In this unit you will:

- learn more phonemic symbols representing consonant sounds
- practise recognizing and producing these consonant sounds
- learn where to place the stress in words with two syllables

In Unit 3, you started to look at consonant sounds with problematic pronunciation. You will now look at some more voiced and unvoiced consonants and think about word stress patterns for two-syllable words.

## Consonant sounds

In this unit you will focus on the consonants shaded in this table.

| /p/ | /t/ | /k/ | /s/ | /ʃ/ | /tʃ/ | /f/ | /θ/ |
|---|---|---|---|---|---|---|---|
| post | take | keep | snow | shoe | choice | leaf | thin |
| /b/ | /d/ | /g/ | /z/ | /ʒ/ | /dʒ/ | /v/ | /ð/ |
| book | doctor | goal | zero | measure | jump | leave | the |
| /h/ | /m/ | /n/ | /ŋ/ | /l/ | /r/ | /w/ | /j/ |
| hotel | meet | nine | bring | late | red | well | yes |

| Task 1 | /ʒ/ **leisure** |
|---|---|

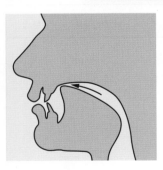

/ʒ/ is voiced, e.g., measure. It is similar to /ʃ/, which is unvoiced, e.g., mesh. For both sounds, the tongue is held close to the roof of the mouth. There is a narrow gap through which you force air. Compare these to sounds /s/ and /z/ on page 27. You will see the tongue is higher and further back in the mouth.

Words ending ~*sion* are sometimes pronounced /~ʒən/ and sometimes /~ʃən/.

1.1 ▶ **CD1: 47 Listen to the pronunciation of the words in the box and write them under the correct heading in the table.**

| decision | version | dimension | occasion | conclusion | discussion |
| expression | admission | expansion | supervision | confusion | erosion |

| /~ʒən/ | /~ʃən/ |
| --- | --- |
|  |  |

Before checking your answers, try and see a pattern in the spelling that helps you decide how ~*sion* is pronounced.

Words ending ~*sure* are sometimes pronounced /~ʒə/, sometimes /~ʃə/, and sometimes /~ʃɔː/.

1.2 ▶ **CD1: 48 Listen to the pronunciation of the words in the box. Write them in the correct column of the table, according to the pronunciation of the word endings.**

| measure | pressure | closure | assure |
| ensure | pleasure | leisure | exposure |

| /~ʒə/ | /~ʃə/ | /~ʃɔː/ |
| --- | --- | --- |
|  |  |  |

**Note:** The pattern in the spelling of words ending in ~*sure* is also similar to that of Ex 1.1. Words which include the letters ~*sual* also usually follow the pattern in Ex 1.1 and 1.2.

1.3 ▶ **CD1: 49 Listen and repeat the following words.**

| visual | casual | usually | sensual |

| Task 2 | /v/ <u>v</u>an |
|---|---|

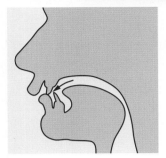

/v/ is voiced, e.g., <u>v</u>ast. It is similar to /f/, which is unvoiced, e.g., *fast*. For both these sounds, the inside part of the bottom lip is held against the top teeth. Pressure is released as you bring the bottom lip away from the top teeth.

**2.1**  ▶ **CD1: 50 Listen to and repeat the words and phrases in the box.**

| visit | develop | value | average | village |
|---|---|---|---|---|
| very good service | violent | every level | voice | When does it arrive? |

**2.2**  ▶ **CD1: 50 Listen and repeat again, this time recording your pronunciation. Play back the recording and evaluate your pronunciation. How accurate is it?**

> **➤ Pronunciation note ◄**

If you find the /v/ sound difficult to pronounce, people should still understand if you replace it with the /f/ sound (and not the /w/ sound).

| So, if you can't say … | try saying … |
|---|---|
| vast | fast |
| view | few |
| invest | infest |
| service | surface |

**2.3**  **If you had problems pronouncing /v/, do Ex 2.1 again, replacing /v/ with /f/.**

| Task 3 | /j/ <u>y</u>et, <u>y</u>ellow, <u>u</u>niversity |
|---|---|

**3.1**  ▶ **CD1: 51 The /j/ sound appears at the beginning of words starting with *y~*. Listen and repeat.**

| yet | young | yellow | year | yesterday |
|---|---|---|---|---|

**3.2** ▶ **CD1: 52 The /j/ sound also appears at the beginning of some words starting with *u~*. Tick (✔) the words below that are pronounced /juː~/.**

1. ✔ union
2. ☐ unless
3. ☐ uniform
4. ☐ uncle
5. ☐ unclear
6. ☐ unique

7. ☐ useful
8. ☐ username
9. ☐ usual
10. ☐ uranium
11. ☐ until
12. ☐ urgent

▶ **CD1: 52 Check your answers, listen and repeat the words.**

**Note:** The negative forms of adjectives, e.g., *unimportant, unlikely,* are pronounced /ʌn~/.

**3.3** ▶ **CD1: 53 You also find the /j/ sound in the middle of words, represented by *y*.**

| beyond | layer | layout | buyer |
|---|---|---|---|

**3.4** ▶ **CD1: 54 Sometimes, the /j/ sound in the middle of words is not represented by any letter. Listen to these words and mark the position of the /j/ sound.**

**Examples:**

n$^j$ew    contin$^j$ue    comp$^j$uter

1. f u e l
2. v i e w
3. a r g u e
4. e d u c a t i o n
5. c u b e

6. f e w
7. r e s c u e
8. d i s t r i b u t e
9. a s s u m e

▶ **CD1: 54 Listen again and repeat the words.**

| Task 4 | /ʃ/ and /tʃ/ <u>sh</u>op, <u>ch</u>op |
|---|---|

When you make the /ʃ/ sound, the air should pass freely around your tongue, which should not touch the roof of your mouth. For the /tʃ/ sound, the tongue touches the roof of the mouth for the /t/ sound before the air passes from the mouth as in /ʃ/.

These sounds are both unvoiced. If you have problems with the /tʃ/ sound, practise saying /t/ before /ʃ/ and then bring the sounds together.

**4.1**  ▶ **CD1: 55 Listen to the difference in pronunciation between these pairs of words.**

| /ʃ/ | /tʃ/ |
|---|---|
| ship | chip |
| shop | chop |
| share | chair |
| shoes | choose |
| cash | catch |
| washed | watched |
| dishes | ditches |

▶ **CD1: 55 Listen again and repeat the words.**

> ➤ **Pronunciation note** ◄
>
> /ʃ/ is usually written as *sh* (*show*, *wash*).
>
> /tʃ/ is usually written as *ch* (*cheap*, *rich*) or as *tch* (*watch*).

**4.2**  ▶ **CD1: 56 You will hear some of the words from Ex 4.1. Circle the phonemic transcription that matches the pronunciation of the word you hear.**

1. /ʃɒp/     (/tʃɒp/)
2. /kæʃ/     /kætʃ/
3. /ʃuːz/     /tʃuːz/
4. /wɒʃd/     /wɒtʃt/
5. /ʃeə/     /tʃeə/
6. /dɪʃɪz/     /dɪtʃɪz/
7. /ʃɪp/     /tʃɪp/

**4.3** **Complete these sentences with words from Ex 4.1.**

1. There's a small _____ on the card which stores your personal data.

2. You can pay with _____ or by cheque.

3. Farmers need to dig _____ to drain the soil.

4. The _____ value has shot up by 30 per cent!

5. You can _____ which topic to write about for your assignment.

6. The sample should be _____ in a five per cent saline solution before analysis.

**4.4** ▶ **CD1: 57 Listen to the correct answers and repeat the sentences.**

| Task 5 | /tʃ/ and /dʒ/ <u>ch</u>oice, <u>j</u>ump |
|---|---|

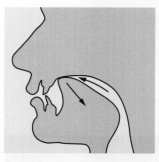 /tʃ/ is voiced, e.g., *choice*. It is similar to /dʒ/, e.g., *jump*, which is unvoiced. For both sounds the tip and sides of the tongue are held against the roof of the mouth, not far from the top teeth. Pressure is released as you bring the tongue away from the roof of the mouth.

**5.1** ▶ **CD1: 58 Listen to the difference in pronunciation between these pairs of words.**

| /tʃ/ | /dʒ/ |
|---|---|
| chunk | junk |
| cheap | Jeep |
| H | age |
| search | surge |
| rich | ridge |
| batch | badge |

▶ **CD1: 58 Listen again and repeat the words.**

> ➤ **Pronunciation note** ◄

/dʒ/ is sometimes written as *j* (*join*, *jump*) and sometimes as *g* (*general*, *imagine*).

*g* is also often pronounced /g/ (*begin*, *girl*, *give*).

**5.2**   ▶ **CD1: 59 You will hear some of the words from Ex 5.1. Circle the phonemic transcription that matches the pronunciation of the word you hear.**

1. (/sɜːtʃ/)        /sɜːdʒ/
2. /rɪtʃ/          /rɪdʒ/
3. /eɪdʒ/          /eɪtʃ/
4. /tʃʌnk/          /dʒʌnk/
5. /bætʃ/          /bædʒ/
6. /tʃiːp/          /dʒiːp/

**5.3**   **Complete these sentences with words from Ex 5.1.**

1. Most fruit and vegetables are _____ in vitamins.
2. Credit card bills are generally prepared by _____ processing of data.
3. A large _____ of the budget is spent on overheads.
4. There is a _____ of high pressure running from northwest to southeast.
5. Children today eat too much _____ food.
6. A sudden _____ in the power supply can damage your computer.

   ▶ **CD1: 60 Listen to the correct answers and repeat the sentences.**

---

| Task 6 | Word stress on two-syllable words |
| --- | --- |

**6.1**   ▶ **CD1: 61 Put the words into the correct column according to their stress pattern.**

| provide | system | assist | reason | prepare | appear |
| --- | --- | --- | --- | --- | --- |
| recent | receive | include | certain | factor | question |
| problem | modern | suggest | reduce | private | observe |

| Oo | oO |
| --- | --- |
| question | provide |
| | |

**6.2**   ▶ **CD1: 62 Listen to these pairs of sentences and mark the syllable stress on the underlined words.**

1. Coffee is this country's biggest 'export.
   They ex'port coffee mainly to Europe.

2. There has been a significant <u>increase</u> in unemployment.
   It has been decided to <u>increase</u> the interest rate by a quarter of a per cent.

3. You need to keep a <u>record</u> of all the references you use in the essay.
   She wants to <u>record</u> the lecture with her MP3 Player.

4. About 30 people were <u>present</u> at the seminar.
   He plans to <u>present</u> the results of his research at the conference.

**Now study the answers to this exercise and Ex 6.1. Can you see a pattern in the spelling?**

6.3 **Complete the explanation of the 'rules' for word stress in two-syllable words, using the words in the box.**

| nouns | verbs | adjectives |
|---|---|---|

Most two-syllable _____ and _____ have stress on the first syllable.

Most two-syllable _____ have stress on the second syllable.

Two-syllable words do not always conform to the rule in Ex 6.3. The stress in words ending in ~er, ~ry, ~le, ~ion, ~age, ~ish, ~ow and ~us generally falls on the first syllable whether they are verbs, nouns or adjectives.

6.4 ▶ **CD1: 63 Listen and repeat these words.**

| ~er | ~ry | ~le | ~ion |
|---|---|---|---|
| answer | angry | angle | action |
| gather | hurry | handle | mention |
| matter | story | middle | nation |
| suffer | vary | trouble | question |
| **~age** | **~ish** | **~ow** | **~us** |
| damage | English | follow | focus |
| language | finish | narrow | minus |
| manage | publish | shadow | |
| package | rubbish | window | |

**Note:** The words *prefer, refer* and *allow* are some exceptions to this rule; they all have stress on the second syllable.

## Unit summary

In this unit, you have learnt six English consonant sounds: /ʃ/, /tʃ/, /ʒ/, /dʒ/, /v/, /j/, and practised their pronunciation. You have also become more aware of sentence stress and how it is used to highlight important information.

**1** **Each of the words in the box contains one of the consonant sounds in the table. Write them in the correct column below.**

| confusion | choices | unusual | system | average |
| service | distribution | innovation | watched | suggest |

| /ʃ/ | /tʃ/ | /dʒ/ | /ʒ/ | /s/ |
|---|---|---|---|---|
|  |  |  |  |  |

**2** **Practise saying the words from Ex 1 and decide which words also contain other consonant sounds that you have studied in this unit (/v/ and /j/).**

**3** ▶ **CD1: 64 Listen to the following pairs of sentences, which contain underlined words with the same spelling. Mark the stressed syllable in each pair of words. In which pairs is the word stress the same, and for which is it different?**

a.  The contracts were signed last week.
    The metal contracts as it cools down.

b.  It caused a lot of damage.
    How does it damage your health?

c.  Why did they object to the proposal?
    Archaeologists are not sure what this object was used for.

d.  What is the main focus of your research?
    We need to focus on the real issues.

For web resources relevant to this book, see:
**www.englishforacademicstudy.com**

This weblink will provide you with further practice in areas of pronunciation such as the sounds, stress and intonation patterns of English.

# 5 Diphthongs 1, sounds in connected speech

In this unit you will:

- learn which phonemic symbols represent certain diphthongs
- practise recognizing and producing diphthongs
- learn how the pronunciation of words is affected by their context in **connected speech**

In Units 1 and 2, you looked at the pronunciation of pure vowels. You will now compare some of these vowels with diphthongs, and study the pronunciation and spelling patterns of high-frequency diphthongs and vowels. You will also become more aware of how sounds change when they are used in a stream of connected speech.

## Diphthongs

Diphthongs can be thought of as a combination of two vowels. When a pure vowel is pronounced, the tongue does not move, but with a diphthong, the tongue moves from the first vowel sound to the second (which receives more emphasis). For example, the /eɪ/ sound in *day* starts as /æ/ and then ends /ɪ/.

In this unit you will focus on the diphthongs shaded in this table.

| /aɪ/ | /aʊ/ | /əʊ/ | /eɪ/ | /eə/ | /ɪə/ | /ɔɪ/ | /ʊə/ |
|------|------|------|------|------|------|------|------|
| wh<u>y</u> | n<u>ow</u> | g<u>o</u> | d<u>ay</u> | c<u>are</u> | d<u>ear</u> | enj<u>oy</u> | p<u>ure</u> |

| Task 1 | /aɪ/ and /ɪ/ wh<u>y</u>, b<u>i</u>g |
|--------|-----------------------------|

1.1 ▶ **CD2: 1 Put the words in the box into the correct column, according to the pronunciation of the vowel or diphthong sound.**

| time | think | life | write | while | win | high | try |
|------|-------|------|-------|-------|-----|------|-----|
| sit | site | buy | bit | might | sign | like | |

| /aɪ/ | /ɪ/ |
|------|-----|
|  |  |

> ➤ **Pronunciation note** ◄

(C = consonant)

The /aɪ/ sound often occurs in:
- one-syllable words ending ~iCe: *fine, rise, drive*
- words including Cigh: *light, fight, thigh*
- one-syllable words written CCy: *why, sky, dry*

The /ɪ/ sound:
- is often written CiC: *lid, fit, ship*
- often occurs in unstressed syllables: *de͞cide, mi͞nute (n).*

However, there are exceptions to these patterns, e.g., *give, live* (v).

**1.2**  **Check how your answers to Ex 1.1 fit these patterns.**

**1.3**  ▶ **CD2: 2 How do you pronounce *l-i-v-e* in each of these sentences?**

1. Where do you live?
2. The match is being shown live on TV.

Why is the pronunciation different in each sentence?

**1.4**  ▶ **CD2: 3 Listen to the words and do activities a and b.**
a. Circle the phonemic transcription that matches the pronunciation of the word you hear.

| | | | | |
|---|---|---|---|---|
| 1. | /wɪl/ | _____ | /waɪl/ | _____ |
| 2. | /fɪt/ | _____ | /faɪt/ | _____ |
| 3. | /stɪl/ | _____ | /staɪl/ | _____ |
| 4. | /hɪt/ | _____ | /haɪt/ | _____ |
| 5. | /lɪtə/ | _____ | /laɪtə/ | _____ |
| 6. | /hɪd/ | _____ | /haɪd/ | _____ |

b. Now write the words, with the correct spelling, in the spaces next to the phonemic transcriptions.

**1.5**  ▶ **CD2: 4 Underline the /aɪ/ sounds in these sentences. Then listen and repeat the sentences.**

1. Try the other side.
2. The height's fine.
3. This type of plant needs a lot of light.
4. There was a slight rise in the share value.

## Task 2  /əʊ/ and /ɒ/ g<u>o</u>, j<u>o</u>b

**2.1** ▶ **CD2: 5 Put the words in the box into the correct column, according to the pronunciation of the vowel or diphthong sound.**

| cost | coast | show | rod | road | grow | lot | load |
|------|-------|------|-----|------|------|-----|------|
| flow | hope | code | cold | not | note | | fold |

| /əʊ/ | /ɒ/ |
|------|-----|
| | |
| | |
| | |

> ➤ **Pronunciation note** ◄

(C = consonant)

The /əʊ/ sound often occurs in:
- one-syllable words ending ~oCe: *drove*, *hole*, *tone*
- words including *oa*: *loan*, *float*, *coat*
- words ending ~*ow*: *throw*, *slow*, *below*

The /ɒ/ sound:
- is often written CoC: *got*, *sock*, *shop*
- is sometimes written *a*: *what*, *wash*, *want*

However, there are exceptions to these patterns:
- *more, some, gone, those*
- *board, abroad, coarse*
- *now, how*

**2.2** **Check how your answers in Ex 2.1 fit the patterns in the *Pronunciation note*.**

**2.3** ▶ **CD2: 6 Listen to the six words and do activities a and b.**

**a.** Listen and circle the phonemic transcription that matches the pronunciation of the word you hear.

1. /kɒst/ _____ /kəʊst/ _____

2. /nɒt/ _____ /nəʊt/ _____

3. /rɒd/ _____ /rəʊd/ _____

4. /sɒk/ _____ /səʊk/ _____

5. /wɒnt/ _____ /wəʊw/ _____

6. /fɒnd/ _____ /fəʊnd/ _____

**b.** Write the words, with the correct spelling, in the spaces next to the phonemic transcriptions.

**2.4** ▶ **CD2: 7 Underline the /əʊ/ sounds in these sentences. Listen and repeat the sentences.**

1. Most of the gold is exported.
2. The hole in the ozone layer is growing.
3. Gross profits were down.
4. Can you cope with the workload?

---

| Task 3 | /eɪ/, /æ/ and /ɑː/ day, plan, car |
|---|---|

**3.1** ▶ **CD2: 8 Put the words in the box into the correct column, according to the pronunciation of the vowel or diphthong sound.**

| plan | plane | dark | face | make | scale | large | lack |
|---|---|---|---|---|---|---|---|
| heart | play | weigh | gain | part | claim | bad |

| /eɪ/ | /æ/ | /ɑː/ |
|---|---|---|
|  |  |  |
|  |  |  |
|  |  |  |
|  |  |  |
|  |  |  |
|  |  |  |
|  |  |  |

> **➤ Pronunciation note ◄**

(C = consonant)

The /eɪ/ sound often occurs in:
- one-syllable words ending ~aCe: *place, rate, save*
- words ending ~ay: *away, stay, today*
- one-syllable words with *ai*: *paint, raise, train*

The /ɑː/ sound is often written *ar*, but the *r* is often silent in British English: *far, start, hard*.

However, there are exceptions to these patterns, e.g., *have, care*.

**3.2** **Check how your answers to Ex 3.1 fit the patterns in the *Pronunciation note*.**

3.3　▶ **CD2: 9 Listen to the words and do activities a and b.**

a. Circle the phonemic transcription that matches the pronunciation of the word you hear.

1. /læk/ _____ /leɪk/ _____
2. /tæp/ _____ /teɪp/ _____
3. /plæn/ _____ /pleɪn/ _____
4. /lætə/ _____ /leɪtə/ _____
5. /ɑːm/ _____ /eɪm/ _____
6. /mɑːk/ _____ /meɪk/ _____
7. /pɑːs/ _____ /peɪs/ _____
8. /kɑːm/ _____ /keɪm/ _____

b. Write the words, with the correct spelling, in the spaces next to the phonemic transcriptions.

3.4　▶ **CD2: 10 Underline the /eɪ/ sounds in these sentences. Listen and repeat the sentences.**

1. Can you explain this heavy rainfall?
2. That's quite a claim to make.
3. The future remains uncertain.
4. The failure rate is quite high.

## Task 4　Sounds in connected speech

When you listen to native speakers, you may notice changes in sounds when they string words together. It is important to be aware of how sounds may be dropped, changed or added when words are linked in rapid speech.

4.1　▶ **CD2: 11 Listen to these sentences and exchanges.**

1. The Dean must be aware of the problem.
2. What do we need to solve the problem? A system.
3. What would you like me to do? Assist him.

> ➤ **Pronunciation note** ◄
>
> In rapid, connected speech, the pronunciation of some words is affected by the words and sounds that come before and after them. They can be affected in the following ways:
> - Words may seem to be *joined* together (linking), e.g., A‿system.
> - A sound may be *inserted* between words, e.g., be‿/j/‿aware‿/r/‿of.
> - A sound may *disappear* or be very difficult to hear, e.g., *mus(t) be*; *assist (h)im*.

**Linking: Consonant + vowel**

When one word ends in a consonant sound and the next word begins with a vowel sound (or the other way round), the two words may be linked.

**4.2** ▶ **CD2: 12 Listen to the examples.**

hand‿in

split‿up

complex‿issue

**4.3** ▶ **CD2: 13 Listen to these phrases and repeat them, linking the words together where indicated.**

1. divide‿in two
2. historical‿evidence
3. as soon‿as possible
4. take‿over‿control
5. it'll‿end next week

6. the‿Data‿Protection‿Act
7. a‿wide‿area
8. keep‿up with‿it
9. an‿increase‿in crime
10. the‿main‿aim

**4.4** ▶ **CD2: 14 Listen to this introduction from a talk about home ownership and write in the links between words.**

> In this presentation I'm going to talk about home ownership in the UK. First, I'm going to focus on changes in the patterns of home ownership in the last 20 years, and provide an explanation for these changes. Then I'm going to describe the process of buying or selling a house. Finally, I'm going to try to make some predictions about the housing market.

**4.5** ▶ **CD2: 14 Listen again and repeat the text in sections. Try to link words where this is appropriate.**

**Inserting sounds between words: Vowel + vowel**

When one word ends in a vowel sound and the next word starts with another vowel sound, it is often easier to pronounce if we insert an extra sound– /w/, /j/ or /r/ –between the vowels.

We often insert a /w/ sound between words if the first word ends in a vowel or diphthong pronounced with rounded lips, such as /uː/, /ʊə/ or /əʊ/. In the written form, the first word may end in ~w, ~ue or ~o.

**4.6** ▶ **CD2: 15 Listen to the examples. Then repeat the phrases and see if you can produce the /w/ sound.**

…V$^{/w/}$V… (V=Vowel)

1. slow$^{/w/}$economic growth
2. true$^{/w/}$identity
3. go$^{/w/}$up

We often insert a /j/ sound between words if the first word ends in a vowel or diphthong pronounced with stretched lips such as /iː/, /aɪ/ or /eɪ/. In the written form, the first word may end in ~y, ~igh or ~ee.

**4.7**　▶ **CD2: 16 Listen to the examples. Then repeat the phrases and see if you can produce the /j/ sound.**

…V/ʲ/V… (V=Vowel)

1. carry/ʲ/on
2. high/ʲ/altitude
3. free/ʲ/access

> ➤ **Pronunciation note** ◀

In standard British English (RP), the consonant /r/ is not normally pronounced at the ends of words, e.g., *faster* is pronounced /fɑːstə/. However, the /r/ sound is pronounced if the next word starts with a vowel.

Many speakers of other Englishes, for example American English, do pronounce the *r* in most contexts whether the *r* is followed by a vowel or consonant, e.g., /fɑːstər/. This is also the case for speakers in some regions of Britain.

If the first word ends in the /ə/ sound, we often insert the /r/ sound. In the written form, the word may end in ~er, ~re or ~or.

**4.8**　▶ **CD2: 17 Listen to the examples. Repeat the phrases and see if you can produce the /r/ sound.**

…V/ʳ/V… (V=Vowel)

1. extra/ʳ/income
2. cinema/ʳ/advertising
3. aware/ʳ/of the problem
4. after/ʳ/all
5. faster/ʳ/access

**4.9**　▶ **CD2: 18 Listen to these phrases and decide if a /w/, /j/ or /r/ sound needs to be inserted.**

1. try out
2. agree on this
3. two of them
4. driver error
5. radio operator
6. media event
7. high above the Earth
8. How does this tie in?

**4.10**　▶ **CD2: 18 Listen again and repeat the phrases, inserting the sounds where appropriate.**

## Unit summary

In this unit, you have learnt the phonemic symbols for the diphthongs /aɪ/, /əʊ/ and /eɪ/ and looked at sound/spelling patterns for words that contain them. You have also become more aware of how the pronunciation of words is affected by their context in connected speech.

**1**   ▶ **CD2: 19 Underline the diphthong sounds that you hear in the sentences below.**

   a.   I think I'd like to carry on with life sciences, but I'm also interested in psychology. (aɪ)

   b.   I want to go into social work, so I'm studying sociology. (əʊ)

   c.   He came to Cardiff to give a paper on international relations. (eɪ)

**2**   **Identify the words in the sentences in Ex 1 that would normally be linked. Draw in the links like this:**

   I think I'd like to carry …

   ▶ **CD2: 19 Listen again and check your answers.**

**3**   **Study the words below; they are all from the sentences in Ex 1. Which sounds are normally inserted between them to make them easier to pronounce in connected speech?**

   a.   carry on

   b.   go into

   c.   paper on

**4**   **Practise saying the sentences aloud, using the connected speech features you have looked at in the unit.**

**5**   **Think about the statements. Do you agree or disagree with them?**

   a.   It is more important to be able to hear the difference between English vowel sounds and diphthongs than to be able to produce them all correctly.

   b.   Learners need to be able to understand how English speakers link sounds and words together, but don't need to speak in the same way themselves.

---

For web resources relevant to this book, see:
**www.englishforacademicstudy.com**

This weblink will provide you with further practice in areas of pronunciation such as the sounds, stress and intonation patterns of English.

In this unit you will:

- learn how to pronounce groups of consonants (consonant clusters), at the beginning and middle of words
- learn how to divide up connected speech into **tone units**

You have already looked at individual consonant sounds, but you will now focus on how they are often grouped in **consonant clusters**. You will also start to look at the way connected speech is divided into tone units.

## Consonant clusters

In English, you may find groups of two or three consonant sounds:

- at the beginning of words: _grow_, _square_, _straight_
- in the middle of words: _computer_, _expression_, _congratulate_
- at the end of words: _hoped_, _branch_, _strength_
- across two words: _room number_, _clamp down_

In other languages, there may be a tendency for the pattern to be consonant–vowel–consonant–vowel, and speakers of such languages may find it difficult to pronounce certain consonant clusters.

| Task 1 | Consonant clusters at the beginning of words |
| --- | --- |

1.1    ▶ **CD2: 20 Listen and repeat these groups of words, which all begin with consonant clusters.**

| | | | | |
| --- | --- | --- | --- | --- |
| blame | platform | claim | glass | flexible |
| blind | plenty | climate | global | flight |
| blood | plus | closure | glue | flow |
| brand | practice | create | graphics | fraction |
| break | pressure | crucial | ground | freeze |
| brief | profit | criteria | growth | frequent |
| draw | transaction | quarter | twelve | threat |
| draft | trend | quality | twice | through |
| drop | trigger | quota | twin | throw |
| | | | | shrink |
| | | | | shred |

Note which of these consonant clusters you have problems pronouncing and try to focus on these in future practice.

**1.2**    ▶ **CD2: 21 Listen and complete these sentences.**

**Note:** The missing words all begin with a consonant cluster.

1. It burns with a blue _____.

2. There was a _____ rise in crime.

3. We are on _____ for ten per cent _____ this year.

4. We need a more _____ definition of the term.

5. It's covered with a steel _____.

6. The _____ needs replacing.

7. Its development can be _____ back to the 15th century.

8. The screen went _____.

9. There is _____ evidence for such a link.

10. It's difficult to follow the _____ of his argument.

**1.3**    ▶ **CD2: 21 Listen again and repeat the phrases. Try to focus on the correct pronunciation of the consonant cluster, the correct word stress and the linking.**

**1.4**    ▶ **CD2: 22 Listen and repeat these further examples of consonant clusters that begin with /s/.**

| | | | | |
|---|---|---|---|---|
| scale | sleep | spare | split | straight |
| scheme | slip | spill | splendid | stress |
| scope | slight | speed | stage | strike |
| score | slope | spoil | step | strong |
| screen | smart | specific | store | sweet |
| script | smell | spray | stuff | swing |
| snack | smoke | spread | style | switch |
| snow | smooth | spring | | |

**1.5**    ▶ **CD2: 23 Listen and complete these phrases or sentences.**

**Note:** The missing words all begin with /s/ and a consonant cluster.

1. This machine _____ the brain.

2. Resources are _____.

3. This _____ is under threat.

4. We're making _____ progress.

5. one important _____

6. He _____ paint on the floor.

7. a _____ feeling

8. a bigger _____ of the cake

9. in a _____ condition

10. a _____ floor

1.6 ▶ **CD2: 23 Listen again and repeat the phrases. Try to focus on the correct pronunciation of the consonant cluster, the correct word stress and the linking.**

| Task 2 | Consonant clusters in the middle of words |
|---|---|

2.1 ▶ **CD2: 24 Listen and repeat these words, which include consonant clusters.**

| impress | central | explain | include | abstract |
|---|---|---|---|---|
| comprise | contract | exploit | conclude | construct |
| compromise | control | explore | enclose | distribute |
| complain | entry | explicit | unclear | industry |
| complete | introduce | extract | conflict | illustrate |
| employ | inspect | extreme | influence | |
| sample | transport | | inflation | |

2.2 ▶ **CD2: 25 Listen and complete these phrases or sentences with words from Ex 2.1.**

1. Supplies need to be _____.

2. no _____ reference

3. the _____ infrastructure

4. this _____ with

5. The causes are _____.

6. oils _____ from plants

7. an _____ concept

8. in order to _____ its potential fully

9. It _____ three parts.

10. in _____ cases

2.3 ▶ **CD2: 25 Listen again and repeat the phrases. Try to focus on the correct pronunciation of the consonant cluster, the correct word stress and the linking.**

| Task 3 | **Disappearing sounds in connected speech** |

**3.1**  ▶ **CD2: 26 Listen to these sentences and write in the missing word.**

1. Did _____ tell you?

2. I've added _____ name to the list.

3. Can you put _____ suitcase in the car?

When function words beginning with *h*, like *he, his, him, her*, are *unstressed* and in the *middle* of a sentence, the /h/ sound often disappears.

However, if these words are at the beginning of a sentence, the /h/ sound is usually pronounced, e.g., *He left at four o'clock*.

**Note:** Consonant sounds at the ends of words may also disappear if the following word begins with the same consonant, e.g., *hi(s) suitcase*.

**Contractions of auxiliary and modal verbs**

In connected speech, auxiliary verbs and some modal verbs are often contracted; that is to say, some of the sounds disappear when they are unstressed. Here is a list of some of the most common contractions.

| Full form | Contraction | Full form | Contraction |
|---|---|---|---|
| he is/he has<br>she is/she has<br>they are<br>they have | he's<br>she's<br>they're<br>they've | could have<br>should have<br>must have | could've<br>should've<br>must've |
| it would/it had<br>he would/he had | it'd<br>he'd | is not<br>are not<br>will not<br>cannot<br>would not | isn't<br>aren't<br>won't<br>can't<br>wouldn't |

**Note:**
1. In academic writing, you should use the full forms and not the contracted forms.
2. *He's* might represent *he is* or *he has*, depending on context.
3. *He'd* might represent *he had* or *he would*, depending on context.

**3.2**  ▶ **CD2: 27 Listen and complete the sentences.**

**Note:** There are two or three words missing from each space.

1. Although _____ requested further funding, _____ not certain that the project will continue beyond 2015.

2. The treatment is expensive, and _____ why _____ not very widely available.

3. Another advantage is that _____ lower the costs.

4. In fact, _____ supposed to be checked every six months.

5. We _____ know for sure, but _____ thought that the space probe _____ been hit by a meteorite.

6. Unfortunately, _____ forgotten just how complicated the process is.

7. The Vikings are believed _____ landed in America well before Columbus.

8. The equipment testing _____ been left until the last minute.

In multi-syllable words, vowel sounds and even whole syllables may disappear if they are unstressed.

**Example:**

*Comfortable* is often pronounced /ˈkʌmftəbəl/, so the letters ~or~ are not pronounced.

3.3 ▶ **CD2: 28 Listen to these sentences and cross out the vowels that are not pronounced in the underlined words.**

1. Veg~e~tables are grown on about 60 per cent of farms in the area.

2. Perhaps he's left.

3. Which category does it fit in?

4. She's studying medicine.

5. I'll phone her secretary.

---

> ➤ **Pronunciation note** ◄
>
> In British English vowels or syllables in the middle of words may disappear, but in American English there is a tendency to pronounce each syllable.
>
> **Example:**
> sec-re-ta-ry /ˈsekrəteriː/

**Study tip**

Many online dictionaries include audio recordings of words. You can often choose whether to listen to the British or American pronunciation of these words.

---

3.4 ▶ **CD2: 29 Listen to these sentences and notice the consonant sounds in the underlined words. Cross out the consonants that are not pronounced.**

**Note:** Where you have groups of consonants together (consonant clusters), some consonants may disappear to make it easier to pronounce in normal informal speech.

**Example:**

*next month* is pronounced /neks mʌnθ/, so the letter *t* may disappear.

1. It reacts with sulphur.

2. They'll send back the results on Tuesday.

3. It must be checked.

4. The low election turnout reflects growing apathy towards politics.

5. The engine tends to overheat in particular circumstances.

**Note:** Generally, as in the above examples, the consonants *t* and *d* are only dropped when they are trapped between other consonants, rather than vowels.

| Task 4 | Changing sounds in connected speech |

Where there are groups of consonant sounds together, they may change in connected speech. For example, in the phrase *ten marks*, /ten mɑːks/, the /n/ sound changes to /m/ in preparation for the next consonant sound /m/.

**Note:** It is important to understand these connected speech features when you listen to native speakers, but it is not necessary to produce them yourself. You will be understood perfectly well if your own consonant sounds are separate and distinct.

**4.1** ▶ **CD2: 30 Listen to these sentences and notice the consonant sounds in the underlined words. Circle the consonant sounds that change.**

1. It has some <u>good points</u>.
2. It's <u>in Britain's</u> interest to become more involved with Europe.
3. He spent three years in an <u>open prison</u>.
4. We don't have much <u>common ground</u>.

| Task 5 | Tone units |

In spoken English, we divide up our stream of speech, pausing at regular intervals to make it easier for the listener to follow. These divisions are known as tone units.

**5.1** ▶ **CD2: 31 Listen to someone explaining tone units and sentence stress. Notice how the text is split into tone units.**

> Whereas <u>written</u> English // is split into <u>words</u> // <u>spo</u>ken English is <u>split</u> // into what are <u>known</u> // as <u>tone</u> <u>units</u>. // Each <u>tone</u> unit contains // at least one <u>prom</u>inent <u>syl</u>lable. // <u>If</u>, however, // it contains <u>two</u>, // then it is <u>usually</u> the <u>second</u> // that contains the <u>main</u> <u>sentence</u> <u>stress</u>. // This is the <u>ton</u>ic <u>syl</u>lable // and it is where most of the <u>pitch</u> change // <u>takes</u> <u>place</u>.

**5.2** ▶ **CD2: 32 Listen to part of the lecture entitled *An Introduction to British Agriculture*. Mark the tone units by writing in double slash signs (//) in the right places.**

You will find it helpful to listen for brief pauses and changes in speaker key.

> As a backdrop to all of these activities, particularly after the Second World War, a lot of effort was put into research and development of agriculture in terms of plant breeding, breeding crops that were higher yielding, that were perhaps disease-resistant, and so on and so forth. Also, crops that might have better quality, better bread-making quality, higher gluten content to make them doughy, higher protein content, and so on and so forth. Research, too, and this is again at one of the

university farms, research into livestock production. Understanding how to better manage our livestock, again to make them produce more, certainly, but also to produce and influence the quality of the livestock products, whether that happens to be milk or cheese, come back to that in a moment, or indeed meat.

5.3 ▶ **CD2: 33 Now listen to an extract from the lecture on globalization. Mark the tone units by writing in double slash signs (//) in the right places.**

Now to get to the meat of the lecture, the basic purpose of this lecture is to give you some overview of the kind of contemporary academic and policy debate about globalization and particularly about a very specific, although rather general, debate itself; that is, the debate on the effect of globalization on the role of the state.

So you see on the overhead the lecture's going to be kind of in two parts: the first will be looking at globalization, causes and consequences and more particularly a kind of definition of the discussion of some of the competing conceptions of globalization, that is, you know, what people say it is, so that we can then discuss in some detail hopefully this question of how globalization's affecting the state.

## Unit summary

In this unit, you have focused on the correct pronunciation of consonant clusters at the beginning and in the middle of words. You have also looked at sounds that disappear in connected speech and become more aware of how English speech is divided into tone units.

**1** ▶ **CD2: 34 Listen to how the following words are pronounced. Say the words in each group below. Underline any words that you find difficult to pronounce.**

| | | | |
|---|---|---|---|
| a. spare | spoil | speed | spray |
| b. central | entry | quarter | track |
| c. school | scale | share | scheme |
| d. street | store | stress | straight |
| e. complete | complex | construct | comprise |
| f. abstract | industry | construct | inspect |

**2** **Identify the consonant cluster in each of the words from Ex 1.**

**3** **Decide which word you think is the odd-one-out in each group. There may be more than one possible answer.**

**4** **The following text is feedback on a student's essay. Read the text and do activities a and b.**

a. ▶ **CD2: 35** Listen to someone reading out the essay feedback. Mark the tone units.

*You have got some interesting ideas and make some good points, but you could have developed these a bit more. You must make sure that you check your essay for spelling mistakes and check the grammar is correct. Perhaps you should have asked your tutor to read through your work as he would have helped you improve it.*

b. ▶ **CD2: 35** Listen again and try to read the text aloud as you listen to the recording, paying attention to the consonant clusters, contractions and tone units.

For web resources relevant to this book, see:
**www.englishforacademicstudy.com**

This weblink will provide you with further practice in areas of pronunciation such as the sounds, stress and intonation patterns of English.

# Diphthongs 2, tone units 2

In this unit you will:

- learn which phonemic symbols represent other diphthongs
- practise recognizing and producing these diphthongs
- have more practice identifying sentence stress and tone units

## Diphthongs

In this unit, you will focus on the diphthongs shaded in this table. You will also have additional practice in identifying tone units and stressed words within them.

| /aɪ/ | /aʊ/ | /əʊ/ | /eɪ/ | /eə/ | /ɪə/ | /ɔɪ/ | /ʊə/ |
|------|------|------|------|------|------|------|------|
| why | n<u>ow</u> | g<u>o</u> | d<u>ay</u> | c<u>are</u> | d<u>ear</u> | enj<u>oy</u> | p<u>ure</u> |

| Task 1 | /eə/ and /ɪə/ <u>care, dear</u> |
|--------|--------------------------------|

**1.1** ▶ **CD2: 36 Put the words in the box into the correct column, according to the pronunciation of the diphthong sound.**

| share | fair | mere | square | near | adhere | sphere | year | there |
|-------|------|------|--------|------|--------|--------|------|-------|
| where | aware | appear | severe | wear | pair | chair | bear | fare |

| /eə/ | /ɪə/ |
|------|------|
|      |      |

> **Pronunciation note** ◄

The /eə/ sound is often written:

- ~are: care, prepare
- ~air: hair, repair

The /ɪə/ sound is often written:

- ~ear: fear, gear
- ~ere: here, sincere

However, there are exceptions to these patterns, e.g., wear /weə/, bear /beə/, where /weə/ and there /ðeə/.

**1.2**    **Check how your answers to Ex 1.1 fit the *Pronunciation note* patterns.**

**1.3**    ▶ **CD2: 37 Listen and complete these sentences using words from Ex 1.1.**

1.  As far as I'm _____, there has been little previous research into this issue.

2.  Patients suffering from _____ depression are often treated with drugs.

3.  The _____ fact that they have agreed to negotiate does not indicate that an end to the conflict is near.

4.  These countries needed to _____ for entry into the EMU.

5.  How can we _____ the damage done?

6.  The area of land is about 20 metres _____.

7.  The seeds _____ to the fur of animals, which distribute them over a large area.

8.  We need to _____ in mind that events in South America are largely beyond

    the UK's _____ of influence.

**Listen again and repeat the sentences.**

---

| Task 2 | /aʊ/ and /əʊ/ <u>now</u>, <u>go</u> |
| --- | --- |

**2.1**    ▶ **CD2: 38 Put the words in the box into the correct column, according to the pronunciation of *ow*.**

| allow | crowd | below | own | flow | down | power | growth | now |
| --- | --- | --- | --- | --- | --- | --- | --- | --- |
| know | slow | follow | brown | show | powder | crown | owe | shower |

| /aʊ/ | /əʊ/ |
| --- | --- |
|  |  |
|  |  |
|  |  |
|  |  |
|  |  |

**Note:** The letters *ow* are sometimes pronounced /aʊ/ and sometimes /əʊ/.

**2.2** ▶ **CD2: 39 Underline the words that include the /aʊ/ sound.**

**Note:** The letters *ou* are often also pronounced /aʊ/, but not always.

| loud | doubt | group | account | court | serious | sound | various | trouble |
|------|-------|-------|---------|-------|---------|-------|---------|---------|
| south | amount | colour | course | enough | young | hour | ground | flavour |

**2.3** ▶ **CD2: 40 Listen and complete the sentences, using words from Ex 2.1 and 2.2.**

1. How do we _____ for this increase in temperature?

2. Margaret Thatcher came to _____ in 1979.

3. The new road system is designed to improve traffic _____ through the city centre.

4. The animal feed is usually sold in _____ form.

5. It is without _____ the most _____ crisis the government has faced.

6. You need to _____ 21 days for delivery.

7. Economic _____ has slowed down over the last six months.

8. He is doing research into _____ behaviour.

9. A significant _____ of water is lost through perspiration.

10. The cheese has quite a strong _____.

**Listen again and repeat the sentences.**

---

**Task 3** **/ɔɪ/ enjoy**

**3.1** ▶ **CD2: 41 Listen and repeat the words in the box.**

**Note:** The letters *oi* and *oy* are usually pronounced /ɔɪ/.

| coin | point | join | avoid | soil | noise |
|------|-------|------|-------|------|-------|
| boy | employ | enjoy | royal | annoy | soya |

**3.2** ▶ **CD2: 42 Listen and complete these sentences by writing a word in each space.**

**Note:** Each word includes the letters *oi* or *oy*, but they are not words from the previous exercise.

1. The questionnaire comprises multiple-_____ and open questions.

2. The government is keen for parents to have a _____ in determining how their children are educated.

3. During the civil war, the army remained _____ to the king.

4. The company has _____ a new marketing director.

5. Large parts of the city were _____ in the earthquake.

6. It is often claimed that we fail to _____ scientific developments made in UK universities.

7. Many sailors died during long sea _____ because of poor nutrition.

8. The new company is a _____ venture between Italian and Egyptian _____ companies.

**Listen again and repeat the sentences.**

| Task 4 | Tone units 2 |
|---|---|

4.1   ▶ **CD2: 43 Listen and complete this extract from a lecture on higher education in England and Wales. Write one to five words in each space.**

I'm going to tell you something about the education system before students get to the higher level. There are several reasons for this. One is, of course, it's part of the plan of your course designers to give you the experience of lectures before you go into your real departments in September or October, but another reason is that we have found in the past that many students come to Britain and they live and study here for a year or two and they go away without knowing some of the most basic facts about the education system here.

It's _____ that the education system here, _____ your countries, is changing very rapidly and this means that _____ people, who don't _____ have direct experience, they probably give you information about the education system _____, rather than as it actually is now.

Now what qualifications, _____, do I have to speak on this particular subject? Well, I'm, _____ in the introduction, I'm here at Reading University and my main _____ is to look after international students here, like you, who need academic language support. Now between 20 and 23 per cent of the students in this university, in Reading University, do not have English as their first language and did not receive their previous education in the United Kingdom. So that's a large number of students, _____, _____, almost two and a half thousand students, in this university were not actually educated in the United Kingdom before they came to university so you are amongst many. _____, _____, a minority but you're a very large minority.

**4.2** ▶ **CD2: 43 Listen again and mark the tone units in Ex 4.1 by writing in double slash signs (//) in the right places. Look back to Unit 6, Task 5 for an explanation of tone units.**

**4.3** ▶ **CD2: 44 Listen to these extracts from a lecture titled *Financial Markets and Instruments* and underline the words that take the main sentence stress.**

1. We're going to start by explaining why we need a financial market at all.

2. What is the role that is played by a financial market?

3. What is the rationale for having a financial market?

4. And then we're going to move on and explain some of the instruments that are traded in those markets.

5. I'm going to focus mainly on the stocks, bonds, bills, since these are by far the easiest to understand.

**4.4** ▶ **CD2: 44 Listen again and mark the tone units in Ex 4.3 by writing in double slash signs (//) in the right places.**

## Unit summary

In this unit, you have learnt the phonemic symbols for the diphthongs /eə/, /ɪə/, /aʊ/ and /ɔɪ/ and looked at sound/spelling patterns for words that contain them. You have also had more practice in identifying sentence stress and tone units.

**1** **Each of the words in the box contains one of the diphthongs in the table below. Write them in the correct column.**

| annoy | square | crowd | growth | severe | soya | although | doubt |
|---|---|---|---|---|---|---|---|
| steer | owe | pair | south | bear | avoid | year | |

| /eə/ | /ɪə/ | /aʊ/ | /əʊ/ | /ɔɪ/ |
|---|---|---|---|---|
| | | | | |

▶ **CD2: 45** Listen and check your answers.

**2** **Write three more words for each diphthong. Choose words from the unit or from your area of study.**

**3** **Study the different spelling patterns for each sound. Are there any exceptions to the patterns that you looked at in the unit?**

**4** **Read the statements below and decide whether you agree with each one or not.**

  **a.** English words can be hard to pronounce because there are so many vowel sounds and spelling patterns.

  **b.** Looking at the phonemes for the vowel or diphthong sounds in a new word helps me remember its pronunciation.

  **c.** It is important to understand how native speakers join words together and omit sounds when they speak in English.

  **d.** It is less important for non-native speakers to use connected speech features themselves.

  **e.** It is easier to understand a talk or lecture if you are aware of how the speaker divides his or her speech into tone units.

For web resources relevant to this book, see:
**www.englishforacademicstudy.com**

This weblink will provide you with further practice in areas of pronunciation such as the sounds, stress and intonation patterns of English.

# 8 Consonant clusters 2, intonation

In this unit you will:

- learn how to pronounce consonant clusters at the end of words and across two words
- learn how **intonation** is used to organize and emphasize information

In Unit 6, you studied consonant clusters at the beginning and middle of words. In this unit, you will learn how to pronounce consonant clusters at the end of words and across two words. You will also look at typical intonation patterns in academic discourse.

## Task 1    Consonant clusters at the ends of words

**1.1**    ▶ **CD2: 46 Listen and repeat these groups of words, which end with consonant clusters.**

**Note:** In some cases, you may hear a very short /ə/ between the consonants.

**Example:**
A word like *arrival* may be pronounced as /əˈraɪvl/ or as /əˈraɪvəl/.

| arrival | impact | criticism | depth | branch |
|---------|--------|-----------|-------|--------|
| critical | conflict | mechanism | length | lunch |
| external | affect | organism | strength | launch |
| financial | abstract | tourism | width | bench |
| principal | range | eleven | wealth | |
| assemble | arrange | given | | |
| resemble | change | govern | | |
| | challenge | driven | | |

**1.2**    ▶ **CD2: 47 Listen to these phrases and sentences and write the missing words in the spaces.**

**Note:** All the words end in consonant clusters.

1. in the _____ stage

2. The job has some _____ benefits.

3. I've lost a _____ of keys.

4. a rather _____ surface.

5. It was discussed at some _____.

6. This is a key _____ of his work.

7. He's studying _____ at Leeds University.

8. They can't afford to take such a _____.

9. the _____ of investment controls

10. in the _____ grade

1.3    ▶ **CD2: 48 Listen to the past verb forms in the box and put them in the correct column depending on the pronunciation of ~ed.**

**Note:** Simple past and past participle forms of regular verbs are formed by adding ~ed, and this ending is pronounced /t/, /d/ or /ɪd/ depending on the verb.

| equipped | combined | involved | concluded |
| constructed | depended | developed | expressed |
| claimed | advised | arranged | adapted |
| lacked | finished | | absorbed |

| /t/ or /d/ | /ɪd/ |
| --- | --- |
| | |

> **➤ Pronunciation note ◄**

When the infinitive form ends in /t/ or /d/, you add /ɪd/.

**Example:**

| want | ⟶ | wanted |
| vote | ⟶ | voted |
| avoid | ⟶ | avoided |
| decide | ⟶ | decided |

When the infinitive ends with any other *unvoiced* consonant you add /t/.

**Example:**

| stop | ⟶ | stopped |
| pick | ⟶ | picked |
| push | ⟶ | pushed |

When the infinitive ends with any other *voiced* consonant, vowel or diphthong you add /d/.

| try | ⟶ | tried |
| tag | ⟶ | tagged |
| tamper | ⟶ | tampered |

**Dropping /t/ and /d/ at the ends of words**

In Unit 6, Ex 3.4, we listened to examples of how the consonant sounds /t/ and /d/ are dropped when they are trapped between other consonants. Sometimes reducing or dropping *t* and *d* can make it difficult to distinguish between present simple and past simple verb forms, which means that the examples in Ex 1.4 are likely to sound the same.

**1.4** ▶ **CD2: 49 Listen to the pairs of sentences and decide whether the verbs sound the same or different.**

**1.** a. I watch television every night.
b. I watched television last night.

**2.** a. Many suppliers raise their prices in situations like this.
b. Many suppliers raised their prices when the exchange rate rose.

These examples show that, when listening, you need to compare what you hear to your understanding of the context, to make sure that you correctly decode meaning.

> ➤ **Pronunciation note** ◄

If you find it difficult to pronounce the consonant clusters, try imagining that the final consonant is part of the following word.

For example, if you find it difficult to say *It lacked a clear focus*, try saying *It lack ta clear focus*.

**1.5** ▶ **CD2: 50 Listen and repeat these phrases.**

**1.** arranged at short notice

**2.** the team involved in the project

**3.** constructed in three months

**4.** absorbed into the bloodstream

**5.** the benefits claimed in the report

**6.** we've avoided the problem

**7.** a technique developed in Brazil

**8.** specially adapted equipment

**9.** aimed at a niche market

**10.** enclosed in plastic

---

| Task 2 | Intonation |
| --- | --- |

**2.1** ▶ **CD2: 51 Listen to the following short exchange and decide whether the speaker's voice rises or falls on the underlined words.**

**A:** Has everything been checked?

**B:** Yes, I think so.

**A:** What about the <u>temperature</u>?

**B:** Yes, I've checked the <u>temperature</u>, and it's normal.

If you listen carefully, you will hear that the voice goes down in tone in the first instance **(falling intonation)**, and up in tone in the second instance **(rising intonation)**.

▶ **CD2: 52 Listen to the two words in isolation.**

**A:** temperature

**B:** temperature

**2.2**  ▶ **CD2: 53 Listen to another short exchange and do activities a–c.**

a.  Underline the word that is stressed in each sentence.

   **A:**  It's too expensive.
   **B:**  Well, it's expensive, but it's worth it.

b.  Note whether there is a rising (↗) or falling (↘) tone on the stressed words.

c.  ▶ **CD2: 53** Listen again and check your answers.

---

> ➤ **Pronunciation note** ◄

In English, speakers use intonation for different functions. Two of these functions are:
- to organize and emphasize information
- to show their attitude to the topic under discussion

Like sentence stress, changes of intonation are affected by speaker choice and context. They are not governed by a clear set of rules.

In the exchanges in Ex 2.1 and 2.2, the reasons for the choice of intonation patterns are as follows:
- a <u>falling tone</u>, e.g., ↘ *temperature*, is used when the speaker *introduces a new idea into the discussion*
- a <u>rising tone</u>, e.g., ↗ *temperature,* is used when the speaker *refers to or questions an idea that has already been introduced.* In other words, it is <u>not</u> a new idea in the discussion

In general, a falling tone is characteristic of statements and shows certainty, such as when a conclusion has been reached. In the last sentence of Ex 2.1, the word *normal* has a falling tone to indicate finality: *I've checked the ↗ temperature and it's ↘ normal.*

A rising tone generally signals that something else is coming: that the speaker has not finished or expects an answer from someone else. It is characteristic of information checking and is used in *yes/no* questions.

---

**2.3**  ▶ **CD2: 54 Compare this conversation with the previous one in Ex 2.2.**

**Note:** Even when we use different words to refer back to a previous idea, there is still a rising tone.

**A:**  It's too ↘ <u>expensive</u>.

**B:**  Yes, it's a lot of ↗ <u>money</u>, but it's ↘ worth it.

In this case, *money* has a rising tone, because it refers back to the idea of *expensive.*

**2.4**  ▶ **CD2: 55 Listen to these short conversations. Notice the falling tone for new information and the rising tone for information that is not new.**

1.  **A:**  When's the ↘ <u>deadline</u> for the new building project?
    **B:**  The ↗ <u>deadline</u>? I think it's next Thursday.

2.  **A:**  Why do these prices ↘ <u>fluctuate</u>?
    **B:**  Changes in the exchange rate cause this ↗ <u>variation</u>.

**2.5** ▶ **CD2: 56 Listen to this conversation and mark the falling and rising tones.**

**Note:** The rise or fall starts on the stressed word and continues to the end of the <u>tone unit</u> (see page 59). The first rise has been marked for you as an example. The stressed words are underlined.

A: ↗ Can I <u>help</u> you?

B: Yes, where's the <u>Physics</u> Department?

A: It's on the second <u>floor</u>.

B: On the <u>second</u> floor?

A: Yes, that's right. Take the <u>lift</u> over there.

B: I'm not keen on <u>lifts</u>. I'd rather <u>walk</u> there.

A: Suit yourself. The <u>stairs</u> are down the <u>corridor</u>, on the left.

B: Down <u>there</u>, on the <u>left</u>. Thanks very much!

**2.6** ▶ **CD2: 57 Now take the role of Student B and reply to Student A in the pauses provided.**

A: Can I ↗ <u>help</u> you?
[PAUSE]

A: It's on the second <u>floor</u>.
[PAUSE]

A: Yes, that's right. Take the <u>lift</u> over there.
[PAUSE]

A: Suit yourself. The <u>stairs</u> are down the <u>corridor</u>, on the left.
[PAUSE]

**2.7** ▶ **CD2: 58 Listen to this short extract from a lecture and mark the falling and rising tones on the underlined words.**

In these two lectures, we're going to look at two theories of child development. Firstly, I'm going to look at Jean Piaget. Then, next week, I'll talk about the life and work of Erik Erikson. So this week, it's about Jean <u>Piaget</u>. Now, <u>Piaget's</u> theories were very much influenced by his own <u>experiences</u>, so I'm going to talk about his <u>life</u> and how he developed his ideas, and then I'm going to describe Piaget's four stages of child development.

**What is the lecturer signalling by his use of rising intonation on the underlined words.**

**Note:** When we are listening to lectures, we need to understand how the lecturer signals what he is going to say through his use of intonation.

**2.8** ▶ **CD2: 59 Listen to someone talking about streaming a video from a website. Mark the rising and falling tones on the underlined words.**

> With <u>streaming</u> video, the video is downloaded to your computer as you are
>
> <u>listening</u> to it. And usually you can't <u>save</u> it.
>
> This stops people making copies of the <u>video</u>, <u>editing</u> or <u>pirating</u> it.
>
> The <u>problem</u> is, if you don't have enough <u>bandwidth</u>, or if you're on a network and
>
> it's very <u>busy</u>, your computer won't be able to download <u>fast</u> enough.
>
> As a <u>result</u>, the picture quality is often <u>poor</u>, or the pictures are <u>jerky</u> and sometimes
>
> the video even <u>freezes</u>.

### ➤ Pronunciation note ◀

In addition to falling and rising tones, it is important to be aware of another intonation pattern: the *fall-rise tone*. If you were listening carefully to the previous two recordings, you may have picked this up already. The fall-rise is a more complex tone that invites another person's input. It is thus characteristic of *turn-taking* in a conversation. It also shows mild disagreement or uncertainty, thus showing the speaker's attitude.

**2.9** ▶ **CD2: 60 Listen to the pairs of sentences below and do activities a and b.**

**a.** Tick the underlined sentences that include a fall-rise tone.

**1.** a. <u>Can I help you?</u> I don't think you should be here. ☐

    b. <u>Can I help you?</u> That looks difficult. ☐

**2.** a. <u>I know everything's been checked,</u> but let's check again. ☐

    b. <u>I know everything's been checked,</u> so can we go now? ☐

**3.** a. <u>He's an excellent speaker</u>. I always enjoy his lectures. ☐

    b. <u>He's an excellent speaker</u>. I'm not sure I agree with his ideas though. ☐

**b.** Discuss the attitude of the speaker from the ticked sentences, e.g., polite, uncertain.

**2.10** ▶ **CD2: 61 Listen and consider the function of the fall-rise in the following exchange:**

**A:** We need to improve the ↘ <u>technology</u>.

**B:** But training is just as important as ↘↗ <u>technology</u>.

**A:** That's just your ↘ <u>opinion</u>.

**B:** It's not just an ↘↗ <u>opinion</u>. There's evidence to support it.

Here, the fall-rise is used by Speaker B to indicate a viewpoint that is in some way different to Speaker A's.

## Unit summary

In this unit, you have focused on the correct pronunciation of consonant clusters at the end of words and across two words. You have also looked at how intonation is used to organize and emphasize information.

**1** **Complete the summary below using your own words.**

**Consonant clusters**

- Sometimes consonant sounds can disappear when _____

  _____

  _____

  e.g., _____

- ~ed past forms of regular verbs can be pronounced in three different ways:

  _____

  _____

  e.g., _____

- If you find consonant clusters difficult to pronounce, try _____

  _____

  _____

  e.g., _____

**2** ▶ **CD2: 62 Listen to the dialogue and mark the rising and falling tones on the underlined words.**

**A:** We need to discuss your <u>essay</u>. Can you come to my office at <u>3 o'clock</u>?

**B:** I've got a lecture at <u>3 o'clock</u>. And I think I'm working in the <u>evening</u> …

**A:** How about <u>tomorrow</u>? I'll be there at <u>lunchtime</u>.

**B:** OK, I'll come <u>then</u>.

**3** **Think about what you have learnt about pronunciation while studying this book and try to answer the questions below.**

a. Which aspects of English pronunciation have you become more aware of while working through this book?

b. How has this helped you when you listen to English speakers?

c. Which aspects of your own pronunciation have you worked on and/or improved most?

d. What sort of tasks and exercises have you found most useful?

e. Which aspects of your pronunciation are you still concerned about?

f. What can you do to continue to work on these areas?

For web resources relevant to this book, see:
**www.englishforacademicstudy.com**

This weblink will provide you with further practice in areas of pronunciation such as the sounds, stress and intonation patterns of English.

# Glossary

**Academic Word List (AWL)**
A list of 570 word families that are most commonly used in academic contexts.

**connected speech**
The stream of words that form the normal pattern of spoken language. It is important to note that words are pronounced differently in connected speech than when they are in isolation.

**consonant**
A speech sound made by blocking or partly blocking the air used to make the sound, e.g., blocked /b/ or partly blocked (through the nose) /ŋ/.

**consonant clusters**
Groups of consonants at the beginning, in the middle of or at the end of words, e.g., _grow_, _congratulate_, _tracks_.

**diphthong**
A sound that involves two vowels joined together, e.g., the vowel sound in _why_. A diphthong is treated as one sound and given a single phonemic symbol.

**falling tone/falling intonation**
A downward change in tone (or pitch) that gives the listener more understanding of what the speaker is saying. For example, a downward pitch often indicates that the speaker is giving new information.

**function words**
Words that have no concrete meaning, but convey grammatical relationships between words, e.g., articles, conjunctions, prepositions, etc.

**General Service List (GSL)**
The 2,000 most frequently used words in English.

**intonation**
The way a speaker raises and lowers their tone of voice (or pitch) to clarify meaning.

**microskills**
Skills that contribute to a larger skill. A study of pronunciation provides the speaker with microskills for understanding and producing spoken language, i.e., contributes to the larger skills of listening and speaking.

**phonemic alphabet**
A written set of symbols used to represent the sounds of individual languages.

**phonemic symbol**
A symbol that is used to represent the sounds of individual languages. The main sounds of English are represented by 44 phonemic symbols.

**phonemic transcription**
The use of phonemic symbols to show the sounds in written form. It provides the learner with an indication of how a native speaker would pronounce a word or longer stretches of speech.

**pronunciation**
The way sounds are produced to form speech; it covers the individual sounds, the way some sounds are stressed, and the intonation patterns within utterances.

**rising tone/rising intonation**
An upward change in tone (or pitch) that gives the listener more understanding of what the speaker is saying. For example, an upward pitch often indicates that the speaker is referring to information that has already been introduced.

**sentence stress**
The way certain words in a sentence are spoken with more force, also called _prominence_.

**sound/spelling patterns**
The connection between the sounds of a language and the way it is spelt. English does not have a one-to-one relationship between sounds and spelling, but there are many useful patterns that will help the speaker.

**suffix**
A letter or group of letters that can be added to the end of a word to change its meaning. Words with similar suffixes often have similar stress patterns. Suffixes that come at the end of adjectives, for example, include ~_tial_, ~_cial_ and ~_ical_.

**syllable**
A unit of sound within a word. Each syllable has a vowel at its centre and consonants may 'surround' the vowel. It is also possible to have a syllable with just a vowel. For example, one-syllable words: _post_, _take_, two-syllable words: _provide_, _question_, etc.

## tone unit
A stretch of spoken language that includes at least one prominent syllable which marks the beginning of a change in intonation pattern.

## unvoiced consonant
When pronouncing unvoiced consonants, the vocal chords in your throat do not vibrate, for example /p/, /t/ and /k/.

## voiced consonant
When pronouncing voiced consonants, the vocal chords in your throat vibrate, e.g., /b/, /d/ and /g/.

## vowel
A speech sound made without blocking the air used to make the sound. Variations in vowel sounds are determined mainly by the shape of the mouth, how open the mouth is and the position of the tongue.

## weak form
This form is used when a word is not stressed. Using a weak form often affects the pronunciation, particularly the vowel sounds within the word, e.g., *for* is pronounced /fə/ in a weak form.

## word family
A group of words that have the same basic form and similar meanings. For example, the words *produce*, *product*, *production* and *unproductive* are all in the same word family.

## word stress
This is the way that one syllable in a word is given more force. Stressed syllables are louder and longer than unstressed syllables.

# Unit 1: Vowel sounds 1, word stress and weak forms

### CD1, Track 1
### Ex 1.1

**Listen to the difference in the pronunciation of these pairs of words. In each of them the vowel sound is different.**

**1.**

| | |
|---|---|
| fit | feet |
| dip | deep |
| hit | heat |

**2.**

| | |
|---|---|
| mass | mess |
| band | bend |
| had | head |

**3.**

| | |
|---|---|
| hat | heart |
| match | march |
| pack | park |

**4.**

| | |
|---|---|
| ten | turn |
| head | heard |
| went | weren't |

### CD1, Track 2
### Ex 1.2

**You will hear some of the words from Ex 1.1. Listen and circle the phonemic transcription that matches the pronunciation of the word you hear.**

1. heard
2. park
3. turn
4. mass
5. heat
6. weren't
7. deep
8. head
9. heart
10. band

### CD1, Track 3
### Ex 1.3

**Listen to six more words and do activities a and b.**

1. seat
2. met
3. hurt
4. fur
5. live
6. sad

### CD1, Track 4
### Ex 2.1

**Listen to these examples of one, two, three or more syllable words.**

1. **one-syllable words**

aid

quote

source

fee

2. **two-syllable words**

credit

accept

heavy

equate

3. **three or more syllable words.**

policy

similar

environment

identify

individual

### CD1, Track 5
### Ex 2.2

**Listen to these words and decide how many syllables there are in each of them.**

1. specific
2. alter
3. resource

4. preliminary
5. available
6. consequent
7. framework
8. significant
9. adapt
10. differentiate

## CD1, Track 6
## Ex 3.1

**Listen for the stressed syllable in these words.**

1. policy
2. similar
3. environment
4. identify
5. individual
6. assume
7. major
8. overseas
9. operation
10. reinforce

## CD1, Track 7
## Ex 3.2

**Listen again to the words from Ex 2.2. Mark the stressed syllables as shown in the example.**

1. specific
2. alter
3. resource
4. preliminary
5. available
6. consequent
7. framework
8. significant
9. adapt
10. differentiate

## CD1, Track 8
## Ex 3.3

**Listen to the following sentences and mark the stressed syllable on the underlined words. The first one has been done for you.**

1. The protection of children is the main purpose of this legislation.
2. The samples were analyzed in the lab.
3. Chemical analysis of the rock provided surprising results.
4. The aim of the study was to identify the factors contributing to domestic violence.
5. Periodicals are kept in an area on the ground floor.
6. The administration of these drugs needs to be closely monitored.
7. In percentage terms, this is not a significant increase.
8. This is the standard procedure for limiting the spread of the disease.

## CD1, Track 9
## Ex 4.1

**Listen to these pairs of sentences. What is the difference in the pronunciation of the underlined words in each pair? How can you explain this difference?**

1. a. Interest rates are rising.
   b. No, that's not true. We are doing something about it.
2. a. Would you like some tea?
   b. Most scientists are convinced about global warming, but some are not.
3. a. Where's he coming from?
   b. Results differed from one region to another.
4. a. Is that your pen or mine?
   b. Can I borrow your dictionary?

## CD1, Track 10
## Ex 4.2

**Listen to these sentences and write in the missing words, which are all weak forms of function words.**

1. One criticism levelled at the board was their lack of financial control.
2. This issue was discussed at some length during the conference.

3. These points should have been made more effectively.

4. How do we account for this change in behaviour?

5. This might do more harm than good.

6. This kind of restructuring is usually regarded by employees as a change for the worse.

7. This problem can easily be solved at minimal cost.

8. Trade sanctions will be imposed with effect from the 1st of December.

**CD1, Track 11**
**Ex 4.3**

**Study the following introduction from a lecture on globalization. Listen and write in the missing words. They are all weak forms of function words.**

Well, as Ros said, I'm going to talk about globalization today, which is one of the catchphrases, or buzzwords, if you like, of the late 20th and early 21st centuries. It's constantly in the news. It's used by politicians, by people in the media, by businesspeople, and when they're referring to globalization they talk about things like the way we can communicate almost instantaneously nowadays with people on the other side of the world by e-mail or by television. They're also talking about, for example, the way that a fall in share prices in one part of the world, for example, in the Far East, can have an immediate impact on the stock markets on the other side of the world, like in London or Frankfurt.

**CD1, Track 12**
**Ex 4.4**

**Listen to these phrases and repeat them. Can you identify and produce the weak forms of the function words?**

1. past and present figures

2. more or less fifty

3. they were selected at random

4. it was far from clear

5. the results of the trials

6. too good to be true

7. needless to say

8. it's gone from bad to worse

9. we'll have to wait and see

10. we had some problems

**Unit 1 summary**

**CD1, Track 13**
**Ex 2**

**Now listen to the words from Ex 1 and mark the stressed syllable in each word.**

globalization

century

constantly

politician

refer

media

financial

market

## Unit 2: Vowel sounds 2, word stress patterns

**CD1, Track 14**
**Ex 1.1**

**Listen to the difference in the pronunciation of these pairs of words. In each of them the vowel sound is different.**

1.
match  much

lack  luck

ankle  uncle

2.
pull  pool

soot  suit

full  fool

3.
spot  sport

shot  short

stock  stalk

4.
lock  look

box  books

shock  shook

**CD1, Track 15**

**Ex 1.2**

**You will hear some of the words from Ex 1.1. Listen and circle the phonemic transcription that matches the pronunciation of the word you hear.**

1. lack
2. books
3. pool
4. sport
5. match
6. uncle
7. fool
8. luck
9. stock
10. short

**CD1, Track 16**

**Ex 1.3**

**Listen to six more words and do activities a and b.**

1. fun
2. mud
3. cool
4. bought
5. foot
6. card

**CD1, Track 17**

**Ex 2.1**

**Listen to these examples.**

appear

suggest

effort

colour

**CD1, Track 18**

**Ex 2.2**

**Listen and repeat the words.**

1. computer
2. affect
3. several
4. standard

5. failure
6. purpose
7. propose
8. author
9. attempt
10. distance
11. accept
12. opposite
13. flavour
14. compare
15. approach

**CD1, Track 19**

**Ex 2.3**

**Listen to these examples.**

describe

prefer

**CD1, Track 20**

**Ex 2.4**

c. **Listen and repeat the words.**

1. reduce
2. invited
3. decision
4. demand
5. beyond
6. extensive
7. research
8. interpret

**CD1, Track 21**

**Ex 3.1**

**Listen and repeat the following words, making sure you stress the syllables in the columns highlighted in the tables below.**

**Nouns ending in ~sion or ~tion**

version

solution

occasion

definition

decision

position

**Nouns ending in ~*graphy***

geography

biography

photography

**Adjectives ending in ~*ic***

electric

economic

specific

**Nouns ending in ~*ency* or ~*ancy***

frequency

consultancy

consistency

vacancy

efficiency

redundancy

**Nouns ending in ~*ium***

medium

uranium

consortium

**Adjectives ending in ~*ical***

electrical

political

periodical

**Nouns ending in ~*ity***

identity

authority

community

**Adjectives ending in ~*tial* or ~*cial***

essential

financial

potential

commercial

residential

artificial

**Verbs ending in ~*ify***

modify

clarify

identify

**Nouns ending in ~*logy***

apology

technology

biology

**Adjectives ending in ~*tional* or ~*sional***

additional

international

optional

**CD1, Track 22**
**Ex 3.2**

b. **Listen to check your answers.**
   **Repeat the words to practise your**
   **pronunciation.**

   1. academic
   2. dimension
   3. beneficial
   4. similarity
   5. majority
   6. initial
   7. demography
   8. allergic
   9. tradition
   10. deficiency
   11. conventional
   12. justify

**CD1, Track 23**
**Ex 3.3**

**Listen to check your answers. Practise your**
**pronunciation by playing the recording**
**again and pausing to repeat the sentences.**

1. Most of the course modules are
   compulsory, but there are two optional
   modules.

2. The committee has not yet taken a decision
   whether or not to award funding for the
   project.

3. It is important to start with a definition of
   the term 'sustainable development', as it
   clearly means different things to different
   people.

4. Although solar power provides a potential
   answer to some of the world's energy
   needs, at the moment the technology is
   quite expensive.

5. Have we really found a solution to the
   problem?

6. It is hoped that the development of artificial intelligence will mean that computers will be able to think in the way humans do.

7. There is a lot of confusion, so it is essential to clarify the situation.

8. The stadium was built by an international consortium of construction companies.

9. There is a vacancy for a laboratory technician, so the post will be advertised next week.

10. James Watson's biography of Margaret Thatcher was published last month.

11. The organization plans to publish a new periodical, with three issues a year.

12. Would you like me to bring anything specific to dinner next week?

13. We will need to modify the design of the equipment after a number of weaknesses were discovered in the testing process.

14. Professor Jones is a leading authority on 17th-century Italian literature.

15. The residential areas of the new town will be located well away from the industrial and commercial zones.

## CD1, Track 24
## Ex 4.1

**Listen to the examples.**

| possess | possession | possessive |
| persuade | persuasion | persuasive |
| assess | assessment | assessed |

**However, in some cases the word stress may vary from one form to another.**

| analyze | analysis | analytical |

## CD1, Track 25
## Ex 4.2

**Listen and repeat these words. Mark the stressed syllable. The first one is done for you.**

| apply | application | applicable |
| activate | activity | active |
| inform | information | informative |
| – | probability | probable |
| socialize | society | social |

| experiment | experiment | experimental |
| equal | equality | equal |
| unite | union | united |
| transfer | transfer | transferable |

## CD1, Track 26
## Ex 4.3

**Listen to these examples.**

| occur | occurrence |
| assume | assumption |

## CD1, Track 27
## Ex 4.4

**Listen to the sentences and correct any that you got wrong.**

1. We need to analyze the data.

   Statistical analysis of the data provided some unexpected results.

   You need good analytical skills for this kind of work.

2. The stomach produces acids, which help to digest food.

   The new model should be in production in November.

   If the factory does not become more productive, it faces closure.

   The product was withdrawn from sale after a number of defects were identified.

3. Four alternative methods of payment are offered.

   She takes a very methodical approach to her work.

   They have been developing a new method for research in this area.

4. The president stated that economic development was the main priority.

   The chancellor is concerned that the economy is overheating.

   She is studying economics at Lancaster University.

5. Wages tend to be higher in the private sector.

   This law is intended to protect people's privacy.

   The water services industry was privatized in the 1980s.

6. The heights of plants varied from 8 cm to 15 cm.

   A wide variety of fruit is grown on the island.

   Regional variations in the unemployment rate are significant.

   A number of variables, such as wind speed and direction, humidity and air pressure, need to be considered.

7. Both approaches yielded similar results.

   There are many similarities between the two religions.

   The firefighters resorted to industrial action to settle the dispute. Similarly, railway workers are threatening to strike because of changes in working practices.

## Unit 2 summary

**CD1, Track 28**
**Ex 1**

**Listen to the words in the box. Then match them to the phonemic transcriptions below.**

| other | ankle | pull | shot |
| uncle | pool | short | another |

# Unit 3: Consonant sounds 1, sentence stress

**CD1, Track 29**
**Ex 1.1**

**Listen and repeat these continuous consonant sounds and some words that contain them. What is the difference between them?**

sssssssss, snow, race

zzzzzzzz, zero, raise

**CD1, Track 30**
**Ex 1.2**

**Listen and repeat each pair of words from the table. Can you hear the difference in pronunciation?**

| pie | buy |
| town | down |
| coal | goal |
| sink | zinc |

| mesh | measure |
| chunk | junk |
| fast | vast |
| breath | breathe |

**CD1, Track 31**
**Ex 1.3**

**Listen to the following words and circle the one you hear.**

1. bill
2. paste
3. symbol
4. dense
5. try
6. wide
7. guard
8. class
9. angle
10. zone
11. price
12. use
13. advise
14. rich
15. badge
16. view
17. prove
18. belief

**CD1, Track 32**
**Ex 1.4**

**Listen and complete these sentences or phrases.**

1. a. a tense situation
   b. a dense material

2. a. a wide area
   b. as white as a sheet

3. a. at the base of the plant
   b. the pace of change

4. a. Public services have improved.
   b. A cube has six surfaces.

5. a. difficult to refuse
   b. It's had good reviews.

6. a. the cause of the fire
   b. It changed the course of his life.

## CD1, Track 33
### Ex 2.1

**Listen to the difference in pronunciation between these pairs of words.**

| | |
|---|---|
| thing | sing |
| path | pass |
| worth | worse |
| mouth | mouse |
| youth | use |
| thin | tin |
| thank | tank |
| thread | tread |
| both | boat |
| death | debt |

## CD1, Track 34
### Ex 2.2

**You will hear some of the words from Ex 2.1. Circle the phonemic transcription that matches the pronunciation of the word you hear.**

1. thin
2. tank
3. death
4. both
5. worth
6. pass
7. mouth
8. use

## CD1, Track 35
### Ex 2.4

**Listen to the correct answers and repeat the sentences.**

1. The painting is supposed to be worth £5 million.
2. The fuel is stored in a 30-litre tank.
3. Cancer is the leading cause of death among women.
4. A thin layer of plastic is needed to provide waterproofing.

5. I couldn't follow the thread of his argument.
6. The thing is, no one likes to be criticized.
7. Tax increases are necessary to finance the national debt.

## CD1, Track 36
### Ex 3.1

**Listen and repeat these words.**

| | |
|---|---|
| the | whether |
| this | gather |
| these | either |
| that | neither |
| those | together |
| they | bother |
| their | rather |
| there | other |
| theirs | another |
| than | further |
| then | mother |
| though | father |
| weather | brother |

## CD1, Track 37
### Ex 3.2

**Listen to these sentences and phrases and repeat them.**

1. What's the weather like there?
2. Let's get together.
3. I'd rather not.
4. I wouldn't bother.
5. I don't like them.
6. I don't like them, either.
7. … further down the road …
8. … the other day …

## CD1, Track 38
### Ex 4.1

**Listen to these two words.**

thank

than

**CD1, Track 39**

**Ex 4.2**

**Listen to these phrases and write in the correct symbols above the words.**

1. … another thing to consider is …

2. … in theory …

3. … the truth is that …

4. … the growth rate …

5. … a further theme …

6. … they thought that …

7. … this method …

8. … beneath the surface …

9. … this therapy might be used to …

10. … youth culture …

**CD1, Track 40**

**Ex 5.1**

**Listen to the paragraph. Notice which words are stressed.**

So whose responsibility is it to ensure that children eat healthily? Well, clearly parents have a role, but while children are at school, it's difficult to keep track of what they are eating, so some would suggest that schools need to encourage healthy eating, and that this should be reflected in the menus they offer. Then there's the food industry. They've been criticized in the past for high levels of sugar, fat and salt in food and for not giving clear information on the levels of different ingredients in food. And finally there's the government. Should legislation be used to address this issue?

**CD1, Track 41**

**Ex 5.2**

**Listen to these sentences in which the stress changes according to the meaning. Practise repeating them with the correct stress.**

1. You have to hand in the essay on Monday … there's a strict deadline.

2. You have to hand in the essay on Monday … not the report.

3. You have to hand in the essay on Monday … not Wednesday.

**CD1, Track 42**

**Ex 5.3**

**Listen to the beginnings of the sentences and choose the most suitable ending, according to the sentence stress.**

1. Well, we know how this happened, …

2. Having looked at the effect of deforestation on the environment, …

3. Most of our cotton is imported, …

4. The crime rate fell by 15 per cent last year, …

5. The oil pump needs replacing, …

**CD1, Track 43**

**Ex 5.4**

**Now listen to the complete sentences to check your answers.**

1. Well, we know how this happened, but do we know why it happened?

2. Having looked at the effect of deforestation on the environment, we will now discuss greenhouse gases and the roles they play.

3. Most of our cotton is imported, but we produce about 500,000 tonnes a year.

4. The crime rate fell by 15 per cent last year, but this year it's risen.

5. The oil pump needs replacing, not the filter.

**CD1, Track 44**

**Ex 5.5**

**Read and listen to an extract from a lecture called _Introduction to British Agriculture_. Underline any stressed words that you hear.**

As a backdrop to all of these activities, particularly after the Second World War, a lot of effort was put into research and development of agriculture in terms of plant breeding, breeding crops that were higher yielding, that were perhaps disease-resistant, and so on and so forth. Also, crops that might have better quality, better bread-making quality, higher gluten content, to make them doughy, higher protein content, and so on and so forth. Research, too, and this is again at one of the university farms, research into livestock production. Understanding how to better manage our livestock, again to make them produce more, certainly, but also to produce and influence the quality of the livestock products, whether that happens to be milk or cheese, come back to that in a moment, or indeed meat.

**CD1, Track 45**

**Ex 5.7**

**Read and listen to part of a lecture on globalization. Underline any stressed words that you hear.**

Now to get to the meat of the lecture, the basic purpose of this lecture is to give you some overview of the kind of contemporary academic and policy debate about globalization and particularly about a very specific, although rather general debate itself, that is the debate on the effect of globalization on the role of the state. So, you see on the overhead, the lecture's going to be kind of in two parts: the first will be looking at globalization, causes and consequences, and more particularly a kind of definition of the discussion of some of the competing conceptions of globalization, that is, you know, what people say it is, so that we can then discuss in some detail, hopefully, this question of how globalization's affecting the state.

**Unit 3 summary**

**CD1, Track 46**

**Ex 3**

**Listen and compare your ideas with the recording.**

a. Some species of shark attack people, but most are harmless.

b. There used to be a Chemistry department, but it closed in 2006.

c. The aid provided to the victims was too little, too late.

d. Many banks stopped lending, when the government wanted them to lend more.

## Unit 4: Consonant sounds 2, word stress on two-syllable words

**CD1, Track 47**

**Ex 1.1**

**Listen to the pronunciation of the words in the box and write them under the correct heading in the table.**

decision

version

dimension

occasion

conclusion

discussion

expression

admission

expansion

supervision

confusion

erosion

**CD1, Track 48**

**Ex 1.2**

**Listen to the pronunciation of the words in the box. Write them in the correct column of the table, according to the pronunciation of the word endings.**

measure

pressure

closure

assure

ensure

pleasure

leisure

exposure

**CD1, Track 49**

**Ex 1.3**

**Listen and repeat the following words.**

visual

casual

usually

sensual

**CD1, Track 50**

**Ex 2.1**

**Listen to and repeat the words and phrases in the box.**

visit

develop

value

average

village

very good service

violent

every level

voice

When does it arrive?

**Ex 3.1**

**The /ʝ/ sound appears at the beginning of words starting with *y~*. Listen and repeat.**

yet

young

yellow

year

yesterday

**Ex 3.2**

**The /ʝ/ sound also appears at the beginning of some words starting with *u~*. Tick (✔) the words below that are pronounced /juːn/.**

1. union
2. unless
3. uniform
4. uncle
5. unclear
6. unique
7. useful
8. username
9. usual
10. uranium
11. until
12. urgent

**Ex 3.3**

**You also find the /ʝ/ sound in the middle of words, represented by *~y*.**

beyond

layer

layout

buyer

**Ex 3.4**

**Sometimes, the /ʝ/ sound in the middle of words is not represented by any letter. Listen to these words and mark the position of the /ʝ/ sound.**

1. fuel
2. view
3. argue
4. education
5. cube
6. few
7. rescue
8. distribute
9. assume

**Ex 4.1**

**Listen to the difference in pronunciation between these pairs of words.**

| | |
|---|---|
| ship | chip |
| shop | chop |
| share | chair |
| shoes | choose |
| cash | catch |
| washed | watched |
| dishes | ditches |

**Ex 4.2**

**You will hear some of the words from Ex 4.1. Circle the phonemic transcription that matches the pronunciation of the word you hear.**

1. chop
2. catch
3. shoes
4. watched
5. share
6. ditches
7. chip

**CD1, Track 57**

**Ex 4.4**

**Listen to the correct answers and repeat the sentences.**

1.  There's a small chip on the card which stores your personal data.

2.  You can pay with cash or by cheque.

3.  Farmers need to dig ditches to drain the soil.

4.  The share value has shot up by 30 per cent!

5.  You can choose which topic to write about for your assignment.

6.  The sample should be washed in a five per cent saline solution before analysis.

**CD1, Track 58**

**Ex 5.1**

**Listen to the difference in pronunciation between these pairs of words.**

| | |
|---|---|
| chunk | junk |
| cheap | Jeep |
| H | age |
| search | surge |
| rich | ridge |
| batch | badge |

**CD1, Track 59**

**Ex 5.2**

**You will hear some of the words from Ex 5.1. Circle the phonemic transcription that matches the pronunciation of the word you hear.**

1.  search
2.  ridge
3.  age
4.  chunk
5.  batch
6.  Jeep

**CD1, Track 60**

**Ex 5.3**

**Listen to the correct answers and repeat the sentences.**

1.  Most fruit and vegetables are rich in vitamins.

2.  Credit card bills are generally prepared by batch processing of data.

3.  A large chunk of the budget is spent on overheads.

4.  There is a ridge of high pressure running from northwest to southeast.

5.  Children today eat too much junk food.

6.  A sudden surge in the power supply can damage your computer.

**CD1, Track 61**

**Ex 6.1**

**Put the words into the correct column according to their stress pattern.**

provide

system

assist

reason

prepare

appear

recent

receive

include

certain

factor

question

problem

modern

suggest

reduce

private

observe

**CD1, Track 62**

**Ex 6.2**

**Listen to these pairs of sentences and mark the syllable stress on the underlined words.**

1.  Coffee is this country's biggest export. They export coffee mainly to Europe.

2.  There has been a significant increase in unemployment. It has been decided to increase the interest rate by a quarter of a per cent.

3.  You need to keep a record of all the references you use in the essay.

She wants to record the lecture with her MP3 Player.

4.  About 30 people were present at the seminar.
    He plans to present the results of his research at the conference.

### CD1, Track 63
### Ex 6.4

**Listen and repeat these words.**

answer

gather

matter

suffer

angry

hurry

story

vary

angle

handle

middle

trouble

action

mention

nation

question

damage

language

manage

package

English

finish

publish

rubbish

follow

narrow

shadow

window

focus

minus

## Unit 4 summary

### CD1, Track 64
### Ex 3

**Listen to the following pairs of sentences, which contain underlined words with the same spelling. Mark the stressed syllable in each pair of words. In which pairs is the word stress the same, and for which is it different?**

a.  The contracts were signed last week.
    The metal contracts as it cools down.
b.  It caused a lot of damage.
    How does it damage your health?
c.  Why did they object to the proposal?
    Archaeologists are not sure what this object was used for.
d.  What is the main focus of your research?
    We need to focus on the real issues.

## Unit 5: Diphthongs 1, sounds in connected speech

### CD2, Track 1
### Ex 1.1

**Put the words in the box into the correct column, according to the pronunciation of the vowel or diphthong sound.**

time

think

life

write

while

win

high

try

sit

site

buy

bit

might

sign

like

**CD2, Track 2**

**Ex 1.3**

**How do you pronounce *l-i-v-e* in each of these sentences?**

1. Where do you live?

2. The match is being shown live on TV.

**CD2, Track 3**

**Ex 1.4**

**Listen to the words and do activities a and b.**

1. while

2. fit

3. style

4. height

5. litter

6. hide

**CD2, Track 4**

**Ex 1.5**

**Underline the /aɪ/ sounds in these sentences. Then listen and repeat the sentences.**

1. Try the other side.

2. The height's fine.

3. This type of plant needs a lot of light.

4. There was a slight rise in the share value.

**CD2, Track 5**

**Ex 2.1**

**Put the words in the box into the correct column, according to the pronunciation of the vowel or diphthong sound.**

cost

coast

show

rod

road

grow

lot

load

flow

hope

code

cold

not

note

fold

**CD2, Track 6**

**Ex 2.3**

**Listen to the six words and do activities a and b.**

1. coast

2. not

3. rod

4. soak

5. won't

6. fond

**CD2, Track 7**

**Ex 2.4**

**Underline the /əʊ/ sounds in these sentences. Listen and repeat the sentences.**

1. Most of the gold is exported.

2. The hole in the ozone layer is growing.

3. Gross profits were down.

4. Can you cope with the workload?

**CD2, Track 8**

**Ex 3.1**

**Put the words in the box into the correct column, according to the pronunciation of the vowel or diphthong sound.**

plan

plane

dark

face

make

scale

large

lack

heart

play

weigh

gain

part

claim

bad

**CD2, Track 9**
**Ex 3.3**

**Listen to the words and do activities a and b.**

1. lack
2. tape
3. plan
4. latter
5. aim
6. mark
7. pace
8. came

**CD2, Track 10**
**Ex 3.4**

**Underline the /eɪ/ sounds in these sentences. Listen and repeat the sentences.**

1. Can you explain this heavy rainfall?
2. That's quite a claim to make.
3. The future remains uncertain.
4. The failure rate is quite high.

**CD2, Track 11**
**Ex 4.1**

**Listen to these sentences and exchanges.**

1. The Dean must be aware of the problem.
2. What do we need to solve the problem? A system.
3. What would you like me to do? Assist him.

**CD2, Track 12**
**Ex 4.2**

**Listen to the examples.**

hand in

split up

complex issue

**CD2, Track 13**
**Ex 4.3**

**Listen to these phrases and repeat them, linking the words together where indicated.**

1. divide in two
2. historical evidence
3. as soon as possible
4. take over control
5. it'll end next week
6. the Data Protection Act
7. a wide area
8. keep up with it
9. an increase in crime
10. the main aim

**CD2, Track 14**
**Ex 4.4**

**Listen to this introduction from a talk about home ownership and write in the links between words.**

In this presentation I'm going to talk about home ownership in the UK. First, I'm going to focus on changes in the patterns of home ownership in the last 20 years, and provide an explanation for these changes. Then I'm going to describe the process of buying or selling a house. Finally, I'm going to try to make some predictions about the housing market.

**CD2, Track 15**
**Ex 4.6**

**Listen to the examples. Then repeat the phrases and see if you can produce the /w/ sound.**

1. slow economic growth
2. true identity
3. go up

**CD2, Track 16**
**Ex 4.7**

**Listen to the examples. Then repeat the phrases and see if you can produce the /j/ sound.**

1. carry on
2. high altitude
3. free access

**CD2, Track 17**

**Ex 4.8**

**Listen to the examples. Repeat the phrases and see if you can produce the /r/ sound.**

1. extra income
2. cinema advertising
3. aware of the problem
4. after all
5. faster access

**CD2, Track 18**

**Ex 4.9**

**Listen to these phrases and decide if a /w/, /j/ or /r/ sound needs to be inserted.**

1. try out
2. agree on this
3. two of them
4. driver error
5. radio operator
6. media event
7. high above the Earth
8. How does this tie in?

**Unit 5 summary**

**CD2, Track 19**

**Ex 1**

**Underline the diphthong sounds that you hear in the sentences below.**

a. I think I'd like to carry on with life sciences, but I'm also interested in psychology.
b. I want to go into social work, so I'm studying sociology.
c. He came to Cardiff to give a paper on international relations.

## Unit 6: Consonant clusters 1, tone units 1

**CD2, Track 20**

**Ex 1.1**

**Listen and repeat these groups of words, which all begin with consonant clusters.**

blame
blind
blood

brand
break
brief

draw
draft
drop

platform
plenty
plus

practice
pressure
profit

transaction
trend
trigger

claim
climate
closure

create
crucial
criteria

quarter
quality
quota

glass
global
glue

graphics
ground
growth

twelve
twice
twin

flexible
flight
flow

fraction
freeze
frequent

threat
through
throw

shrink
shred

**CD2, Track 21**
**Ex 1.2**

**Listen and complete these sentences.**

1. It burns with a blue flame.
2. There was a gradual rise in crime.
3. We are on track for ten per cent growth this year.
4. We need a more precise definition of the term.
5. It's covered with a steel plate.
6. The drum needs replacing.
7. Its development can be traced back to the 15th century.
8. The screen went blank.
9. There is fresh evidence for such a link.
10. It's difficult to follow the thread of his argument.

**CD2, Track 22**
**Ex 1.4**

**Listen and repeat these further examples of consonant clusters that begin with** /s/.
scale
scheme
scope
score

screen
script

snack
snow

sleep
slip
slight
slope

smart
smell

smoke
smooth

spare
spill
speed
spoil
specific

spray
spread
spring
split
splendid

stage
step
store
stuff
style

straight
stress
strike
strong

sweet
swing
switch

**CD2, Track 23**
**Ex 1.5**

**Listen and complete these phrases or sentences.**

1. This machine scans the brain.
2. Resources are scarce.
3. This species is under threat.
4. We're making slow progress.
5. one important strategy
6. He splashed paint on the floor.
7. a strange feeling
8. a bigger slice of the cake
9. in a stable condition
10. a stone floor

**CD2, Track 24**

**Ex 2.1**

**Listen and repeat these words, which include consonant clusters.**

impress
comprise
compromise

complain
complete
employ
sample

central
contract
control
entry
introduce

inspect
transport

explain
exploit
explore
explicit

extract
extreme

include
conclude
enclose
unclear

conflict
influence
inflation

abstract
construct
distribute
industry
illustrate

**CD2, Track 25**

**Ex 2.2**

**Listen and complete these phrases or sentences with words from Ex 2.1.**

1. Supplies need to be distributed.
2. no explicit reference
3. the transport infrastructure
4. this conflicts with
5. The causes are unclear.
6. oils extracted from plants
7. an abstract concept
8. in order to exploit its potential fully
9. It comprises three parts.
10. in extreme cases

**CD2, Track 26**

**Ex 3.1**

**Listen to these sentences and write in the missing word.**

1. Did he tell you?
2. I've added her name to the list.
3. Can you put his suitcase in the car?

**CD2, Track 27**

**Ex 3.2**

**Listen and complete the sentences.**

1. Although they've requested further funding, it's not certain that the project will continue beyond 2015.
2. The treatment is expensive, and that's why it's not very widely available.
3. Another advantage is that it'd lower the costs.
4. In fact, they're supposed to be checked every six months.
5. We can't know for sure, but it's thought that the space probe might've been hit by a meteorite.
6. Unfortunately, I'd forgotten just how complicated the process is.
7. The Vikings are believed to've landed in America well before Columbus.
8. The equipment testing shouldn't've been left until the last minute.

**CD2, Track 28**
**Ex 3.3**

**Listen to these sentences and cross out the vowels that are not pronounced in the underlined words.**

1. Vegetables are grown on about 60 per cent of farms in the area.

2. Perhaps he's left.

3. Which category does it fit in?

4. She's studying medicine.

5. I'll phone her secretary.

**CD2, Track 29**
**Ex 3.4**

**Listen to these sentences and notice the consonant sounds in the underlined words. Cross out the consonants that are not pronounced.**

1. It reacts with sulphur.

2. They'll send back the results on Tuesday.

3. It must be checked.

4. The low election turnout reflects growing apathy towards politics.

5. The engine tends to overheat in particular circumstances.

**CD2, Track 30**
**Ex 4.1**

**Listen to these sentences and notice the consonant sounds in the underlined words. Circle the consonant sounds that change.**

1. It has some good points.

2. It's in Britain's interest to become more involved with Europe.

3. He spent three years in an open prison.

4. We don't have much common ground.

**CD2, Track 31**
**Ex 5.1**

**Listen to someone explaining tone units and sentence stress. Notice how the text is split into tone units.**

Whereas written English is split into words, spoken English is split into what are known as tone units. Each tone unit contains at least one prominent syllable. If, however, it contains two, then it is usually the second that contains the main sentence stress. This is the tonic syllable and it is where most of the pitch change takes place.

**CD2, Track 32**
**Ex 5.2**

**Listen to part of the lecture entitled *An Introduction to British Agriculture*. Mark the tone units by writing in double slash signs (//) in the right places.**

As a backdrop to all of these activities, particularly after the Second World War, a lot of effort was put into research and development of agriculture in terms of plant breeding, breeding crops that were higher yielding, that were perhaps disease-resistant, and so on and so forth. Also, crops that might have better quality, better bread-making quality, higher gluten content to make them doughy, higher protein content, and so on and so forth. Research, too, and this is again at one of the university farms, research into livestock production. Understanding how to better manage our livestock, again to make them produce more, certainly, but also to produce and influence the quality of the livestock products, whether that happens to be milk or cheese, come back to that in a moment, or indeed meat.

**CD2, Track 33**
**Ex 5.3**

**Now listen to an extract from the lecture on globalization. Mark the tone units by writing in double slash signs (//) in the right places.**

Now to get to the meat of the lecture, the basic purpose of this lecture is to give you some overview of the kind of contemporary academic and policy debate about globalization and particularly about a very specific, although rather general, debate itself; that is, the debate on the effect of globalization on the role of the state. So you see on the overhead the lecture's going to be kind of in two parts: the first will be looking at globalization, causes and consequences and more particularly a kind of definition of the discussion of some of the competing conceptions of globalization, that is, you know, what people say it is, so that we can then discuss in some detail hopefully this question of how globalization's affecting the state.

## Unit 6 summary

### CD2, Track 34
### Ex 1

**Listen to how the following words are pronounced. Say the words in each group below. Underline any words that you find difficult to pronounce.**

a. spare    spoil    speed    spray
b. central    entry    quarter    track
c. school    scale    share    scheme
d. street    store    stress    straight
e. complete    complex    construct    comprise
f. abstract    industry    construct    inspect

### CD2, Track 35
### Ex 4a

**Listen to someone reading out the essay feedback. Mark the tone units.**

You have got some interesting ideas and make some good points, but you could have developed these a bit more. You must make sure that you check your essay for spelling mistakes and check the grammar is correct. Perhaps you should have asked your tutor to read through your work as he would have helped you improve it.

## Unit 7: Diphthongs 2, tone units 2

### CD2, Track 36
### Ex 1.1

**Put the words in the box into the correct column, according to the pronunciation of the diphthong sound.**

share

fair

mere

square

near

adhere

sphere

year

there

where

aware

appear

severe

wear

pair

chair

bear

fare

### CD2, Track 37
### Ex 1.3

**Listen and complete these sentences using words from Ex 1.1.**

1. As far as I'm aware, there has been little previous research into this issue.

2. Patients suffering from severe depression are often treated with drugs.

3. The mere fact that they have agreed to negotiate does not indicate that an end to the conflict is near.

4. These countries needed to prepare for entry into the EMU.

5. How can we repair the damage done?

6. The area of land is about 20 metres square.

7. The seeds adhere to the fur of animals, which distribute them over a large area.

8. We need to bear in mind that events in South America are largely beyond the UK's sphere of influence.

### CD2, Track 38
### Ex 2.1

**Put the words in the box into the correct column, according to the pronunciation of *ow*.**

allow

crowd

below

own

flow

down

power

growth

now

know

show

follow

brown

slow

powder

crown

owe

shower

**CD2, Track 39**
**Ex 2.2**

**Underline the words that include the /aʊ/ sound.**

loud

doubt

group

account

court

serious

sound

various

trouble

south

amount

colour

course

enough

young

hour

ground

flavour

**CD2, Track 40**
**Ex 2.3**

**Listen and complete the sentences, using words from Ex 2.1 and 2.2.**

1. How do we account for this increase in temperature?

2. Margaret Thatcher came to power in 1979.

3. The new road system is designed to improve traffic flow through the city centre.

4. The animal feed is usually sold in powder form.

5. It is without doubt the most serious crisis the government has faced.

6. You need to allow 21 days for delivery.

7. Economic growth has slowed down over the last six months.

8. He is doing research into crowd behaviour.

9. A significant amount of water is lost through perspiration.

10. The cheese has quite a strong flavour.

**CD2, Track 41**
**Ex 3.1**

**Listen and repeat the words in the box.**

coin

point

join

avoid

soil

noise

boy

employ

enjoy

royal

annoy

soya

**CD2, Track 42**
**Ex 3.2**

**Listen and complete these sentences by writing a word in each space.**

1. The questionnaire comprises multiple-choice and open questions.

2. The government is keen for parents to have a voice in determining how their children are educated.

3. During the civil war, the army remained loyal to the king.

4. The company has appointed a new marketing director.

5. Large parts of the city were destroyed in the earthquake.

6. It is often claimed that we fail to exploit scientific developments made in UK universities.

7. Many sailors died during long sea voyages because of poor nutrition.

8. The new company is a joint venture between Italian and Egyptian oil companies.

## CD2, Track 43
### Ex 4.1

**Listen and complete this extract from a lecture on higher education in England and Wales. Write one to five words in each space.**

I'm going to tell you something about the education system before students get to the higher level. There are several reasons for this. One is, of course, it's part of the plan of your course designers to give you the experience of lectures before you go into your real departments in September or October, but another reason is that we have found in the past that many students come to Britain and they live and study here for a year or two and they go away without knowing some of the most basic facts about the education system here.

It's also true that the education system here, perhaps as in your countries, is changing very rapidly and this means that if you ask older people, who don't actually have direct experience, they probably give you information about the education system as it used to be, rather than as it actually is now.

Now what qualifications, as it were, do I have to speak on this particular subject? Well, I'm, as was said in the introduction, I'm here at Reading University and my main task is to look after international students here, like you, who need academic language support. Now between 20 and 23 per cent of the students in this university, in Reading University, do not have English as their first language and did not receive their previous education in the United Kingdom. So that's a large number of students, that's, you know, almost two and a half thousand students, in this university were not actually educated in the United Kingdom before they came to university so you are amongst many. You are, you know, a minority but you're a very large minority.

## CD2, Track 44
### Ex 4.3

**Listen to these extracts from a lecture titled *Financial Markets and Instruments* and underline the words that take the main sentence stress.**

1. We're going to start by explaining why we need a financial market at all.

2. What is the role that is played by a financial market?

3. What is the rationale for having a financial market?

4. And then we're going to move on and explain some of the instruments that are traded in those markets.

5. I'm going to focus mainly on the stocks, bonds, bills, since these are by far the easiest to understand.

**Unit 7 summary**

## CD2, Track 45
### Ex 1

**Listen and check your answers.**

bear

square

pair

severe

year

steer

crowd

doubt

south

owe

growth

although

avoid

annoy

soya

## Unit 8: Consonant clusters 2, intonation

### CD2, Track 46
### Ex 1.1

**Listen and repeat these groups of words, which end with consonant clusters.**

arrival
critical
external
financial
principal

assemble
resemble

impact
conflict
affect
abstract

range
arrange
change
challenge

criticism
mechanism
organism
tourism

eleven
given
govern
driven

depth
length
strength
width
wealth

branch
lunch
launch
bench

### CD2, Track 47
### Ex 1.2

**Listen to these phrases and sentences and write the missing words in the spaces.**

1.  in the initial stage
2.  The job has some fringe benefits.
3.  I've lost a bunch of keys.
4.  a rather uneven surface
5.  It was discussed at some length.
6.  This is a key aspect of his work.
7.  He's studying journalism at Leeds University.
8.  They can't afford to take such a gamble.
9.  the removal of investment controls
10. in the seventh grade

### CD2, Track 48
### Ex 1.3

**Listen to the past verb forms in the box and put them in the correct column depending on the pronunciation of ~ed.**

equipped

combined

involved

concluded

constructed

depended

developed

expressed

claimed

advised

arranged

adapted

lacked

finished

absorbed

**CD2, Track 49**

**Ex 1.4**

**Listen to the pairs of sentences and decide whether the verbs sound the same or different.**

1. a. I watch television every night.
   b. I watched television last night.

2. a. Many suppliers raise their prices in situations like this.
   b. Many suppliers raised their prices when the exchange rate rose.

**CD2, Track 50**

**Ex 1.5**

**Listen and repeat these phrases.**

1. arranged at short notice
2. the team involved in the project
3. constructed in three months
4. absorbed into the bloodstream
5. the benefits claimed in the report
6. we've avoided the problem
7. a technique developed in Brazil
8. specially adapted equipment
9. aimed at a niche market
10. enclosed in plastic

**CD2, Track 51**

**Ex 2.1**

**Listen to the following short exchange and decide whether the speaker's voice rises or falls on the underlined words.**

A: Has everything been checked?
B: Yes, I think so.
A: What about the temperature?
B: Yes, I've checked the temperature and it's normal.

**CD2, Track 52**

**Ex 2.1**

**Listen to the two words in isolation.**

A: temperature
B: temperature

**CD2, Track 53**

**Ex 2.2**

**Listen to another short exchange and do activities a–c.**

A: It's too expensive.
B: Well, it's expensive, but it's worth it.

**CD2, Track 54**

**Ex 2.3**

**Compare this conversation with the previous one in Ex 2.2.**

A: It's too expensive.
B: Yes, it's a lot of money, but it's worth it.

**CD2, Track 55**

**Ex 2.4**

**Listen to these short conversations. Notice the falling tone for new information and the rising tone for information that is not new.**

1. A: When's the deadline for the new building project?
   B. The deadline? I think it's next Thursday.

2. A: Why do these prices fluctuate?
   B. Changes in the exchange rate cause this variation.

**CD2, Track 56**

**Ex 2.5**

**Listen to this conversation and mark the falling and rising tones.**

A: Can I help you?
B: Yes, where's the Physics Department?
A: It's on the second floor.
B: On the second floor?
A: Yes, that's right. Take the lift over there.
B: I'm not keen on lifts. I'd rather walk there.
A: Suit yourself. The stairs are down the corridor, on the left.
B: Down there, on the left. Thanks very much!

**CD2, Track 57**

**Ex 2.6**

**Now take the role of Student B and reply to Student A in the pauses provided.**

A: Can I help you?
   [PAUSE]
A: It's on the second floor.
   [PAUSE]
A: Yes, that's right. Take the lift over there.
   [PAUSE]
A: Suit yourself. The stairs are down the corridor, on the left.
   [PAUSE]

**CD2, Track 58**

**Ex 2.7**

**Listen to this short extract from a lecture and mark the falling and rising tones on the underlined words.**

In these two lectures, we're going to look at two theories of child development. Firstly, I'm going to look at Jean Piaget. Then, next week, I'll talk about the life and work of Erik Erikson. So this week, it's about Jean Piaget. Now, Piaget's theories were very much influenced by his own experiences, so I'm going to talk about his life and how he developed his ideas, and then I'm going to describe Piaget's four stages of child development.

**CD2, Track 59**

**Ex 2.8**

**Listen to someone talking about streaming a video from a website. Mark the rising and falling tones on the underlined words.**

With streaming video, the video is downloaded to your computer as you are listening to it. And usually you can't save it.

This stops people making copies of the video, editing or pirating it.

The problem is, if you don't have enough bandwidth, or if you're on a network and it's very busy, your computer won't be able to download fast enough.

As a result, the picture quality is often poor, or the pictures are jerky and sometimes the video even freezes.

**CD2, Track 60**

**Ex 2.9**

**Listen to the pairs of sentences below and do activities a and b.**

1.  a.  Can I help you? I don't think you should be here.
    b.  Can I help you? That looks difficult.

2.  a.  I know everything's been checked, but let's check again.
    b.  I know everything's been checked, so can we go now?

3.  a.  He's an excellent speaker. I always enjoy his lectures.
    b.  He's an excellent speaker. I'm not sure I agree with his ideas though.

**CD2, Track 61**

**Ex 2.10**

**Listen and consider the function of the fall-rise in the following exchange.**

A:  We need to improve the technology.

B:  But training is just as important as technology.

A:  That's just your opinion.

B:  It's not just an opinion. There's evidence to support it.

**Unit 8 summary**

**CD2, Track 62**

**Ex 2**

**Listen to the dialogue and mark the rising and falling tones on the underlined words.**

A:  We need to discuss your essay. Can you come to my office at 3 o'clock?

B:  I've got a lecture at 3 o'clock. And I think I'm working in the evening …

A:  How about tomorrow? I'll be there at lunchtime.

B:  OK, I'll come then.

# Answer key

## Unit 1

### Task 1

**Ex 1.2**

1. /hɜːd/ heard
2. /pɑːk/ park
3. /tɜːn/ turn
4. /mæs/ mass
5. /hiːt/ heat
6. /wɜːnt/ weren't
7. /diːp/ deep
8. /hed/ head
9. /hɑːt/ heart
10. /bænd/ band

**Ex 1.3**

1. /sɪt/ sit
2. /mæt/ mat
3. /hɜːt/ hurt
4. /fɑː/ far
5. /lɪv/ live
6. /sæd/ sad

/siːt/ seat
/met/ met
/hɑːt/ heart
/fɜː/ fur
/liːv/ leave
/sed/ said

### Task 2

**Ex 2.2**

1. spe•ci•fic (3)
2. al•ter (2)
3. re•source (2)
4. pre•lim•in•a•ry (5)
5. a•vail•a•ble (4)
6. con•se•quent (3)
7. frame•work (2)
8. sig•nif•ic•ant (4)
9. a•dapt (2)
10. dif•fer•en•ti•ate (5)

### Task 3

**Ex 3.2**

1. spe'cific
2. 'alter
3. 'resource
4. pre'liminary
5. a'vailable
6. 'consequent
7. 'framework
8. sig'nificant
9. a'dapt
10. diffe'rentiate

**Ex 3.3**

1. pro'tection; 'purpose
2. 'analyzed
3. a'nalysis
4. i'dentify; 'factors
5. Peri'odicals
6. admini'stration
7. per'centage
8. pro'cedure

### Task 4

**Ex 4.1**

In general, the underlined words (function words) are unstressed in sentences, and so they are pronounced with the /ə/ sound. Sometimes they are stressed, in which case they are pronounced with their full, strong form.

1. a. /ə/ is unstressed (weak form)
   b. /ɑː/ is stressed (strong form)
2. a. /səm/ is unstressed (weak form)
   b. /sʌm/ is stressed (strong form)
3. a. /frɒm/ is stressed (strong form)
   b. /frəm/ is unstressed (weak form)
4. a. /ɔː/ is stressed (strong form)
   b. /jə/ is unstressed (weak form)

**Ex 4.2**

1. at; of
2. at
3. have
4. for
5. than
6. as; for
7. can; at
8. from

**Ex 4.3**

Well, as Ros said, I'm going to talk about globalization today, which is one <u>of</u> the catchphrases, or buzzwords, if you like, <u>of</u> the late 20<sup>th</sup> <u>and</u> early 21<sup>st</sup> centuries. It's constantly in <u>the</u> news. It's used by politicians, by people in <u>the</u> media, by businesspeople, and when they're referring <u>to</u> globalization they talk about things like <u>the</u> way we <u>can</u> communicate almost instantaneously nowadays with people on the other side <u>of</u> <u>the</u> world by e-mail or by television. They're also talking about, <u>for</u> example, the way that <u>a</u> fall in share prices in one part <u>of</u> <u>the</u> world, <u>for</u> example, in the Far East, <u>can</u> have an immediate impact on the stock markets on the other side <u>of</u> <u>the</u> world, like in London or Frankfurt.

**Ex 4.4**

1. past and present figures
2. more <u>or</u> less fifty
3. they were selected <u>at</u> random
4. it was far <u>from</u> clear
5. the results <u>of the</u> trials
6. too good <u>to</u> be true
7. needless <u>to</u> say
8. it's gone <u>from</u> bad <u>to</u> worse
9. we'll have <u>to</u> wait <u>and</u> see
10. we had <u>some</u> problems

## Summary answers

### Ex 1/2
a. two-syllable words:    ref'er    'market
b. three-syllable words:    'century    'constantly
                              'media    fi'nancial
c. four-syllable words:    poli'tician
d. five-syllable words:    globali'zation

### Ex 3
/ɪ/    politician
/iː/    media
/e/    century
/ɜː/    refer
/æ/    financial
/ɑː/    market

### Ex 4
a. Globalization is one <u>of</u> the buzzwords <u>of</u> <u>the</u> 21ˢᵗ century.
b. It's constantly in <u>the</u> news <u>and is</u> often referred to by politicians <u>and the</u> media.
c. <u>A</u> fall in share prices in one part <u>of the</u> world <u>can</u> have <u>an</u> impact on <u>the</u> stock markets on <u>the</u> other side <u>of the</u> world.

### Ex 5
**Possible answers:**
a. Why do you think learners confuse some of the vowel sounds you have practised in this unit?
   *Students may have fewer vowel sounds in their own language and be unable to differentiate between some English vowels.*
b. Why is it useful to make a note of the stressed syllable when you learn a new multi-syllable word?
   *It will help you remember the stress pattern. You can refer back to your notes if you forget how a word is stressed.*
c. How can you check the correct stress and number of syllables in words that you learn in English?
   *You can check in a good learners' dictionary.*

---

## Unit 2

### Task 1
#### Ex 1.2
1. /læk/ lack
2. /bʊks/ books
3. /puːl/ pool
4. /spɔːt/ sport
5. /mætʃ/ match
6. /ʌnkəl/ uncle
7. /fuːl/ fool
8. /lʌk/ luck
9. /stɒk/ stock
10. /ʃɔːt/ short

### Ex 1.3
1. /fæn/ fan    (/fʌn/ fun)
2. /muːd/ mood    (/mʌd/ mud)
3. (/kuːl/ cool)    /kɔːl/ call
4. /buːt/ boot    (/bɔːt/ bought)
5. (/fʊt/ foot)    /fuːd/ food
6. /kʊd/ could    (/kɑːd/ card)

### Task 2
#### Ex 2.2
**a. and b.**
1. com'puter
2. a'ffect
3. 'several
4. 'standard
5. 'failure
6. 'purpose
7. pro'pose
8. 'author
9. at'tempt
10. 'distance
11. acc'ept
12. 'opposite
13. 'flavour
14. com'pare
15. ap'proach

#### Ex 2.4
**a. and b.**
1. re'duce
2. in'vited
3. de'cision
4. dem'and
5. be'yond
6. ex'tensive
7. re'search
8. in'terpret

### Task 3
#### Ex 3.2
1. aca'demic
2. di'mension
3. bene'ficial
4. simi'larity
5. ma'jority
6. in'itial
7. de'mography
8. al'lergic
9. tra'dition
10. de'ficiency
11. con'ventional
12. 'justify

#### Ex 3.3
1. optional
2. decision
3. definition
4. potential
5. solution
6. artificial
7. clarify
8. consortium
9. vacancy
10. biography
11. periodical
12. specific
13. modify
14. authority
15. residential

## Task 4
### Ex 4.2
a'pply; appli'cation; ap'plicable
'activate; ac'tivity; 'active
in'form; infor'mation; in'formative
proba'bility; 'probable
'socialize; so'ciety; 'social
ex'periment; ex'periment; experi'mental
'equal; e'quality; 'equal
u'nite; 'union; u'nited
trans'fer; 'transfer; trans'ferable

### Ex 4.4
**a. and b.**
1. a'nalysis; ana'lytical
2. pro'duction; pro'ductive; 'product
3. me'thodical; 'method
4. e'conomy; eco'nomics
5. 'privacy; 'privatized
6. va'riety; vari'ations; 'variables
7. simi'larities; 'Similarly

### Summary answers
**Ex 1**
a. /ənʌðə/    another
b. /puːl/    pool
c. /ʃɔːt/    short
d. /pʊl/    pull
e. /ʌŋkəl/    uncle
f. /æŋkəl/    ankle
g. /ʌðə/    other
h. /ʃɒt/    shot

**Ex 2**
Students' own answers.

## Unit 3

### Task 1
**Ex 1.3**
1. bill
2. paste
3. symbol
4. dense
5. try
6. wide
7. guard
8. class
9. angle
10. zone
11. price
12. use (v)
13. advise
14. rich
15. badge
16. view
17. prove
18. belief

### Ex 1.4/1.5
1. a. tense    U
   b. dense    V
2. a. wide    V
   b. white    U
3. a. base    V
   b. pace    U
4. a. services    V
   b. surfaces    U
5. a. refuse    U
   b. reviews    V
6. a. cause    V
   b. course    U

## Task 2
### Ex 2.2
1. /θɪn/ thin
2. /tænk/ tank
3. /deθ/ death
4. /bəʊθ/ both
5. /wɜːθ/ worth
6. /pɑːs/ pass
7. /maʊθ/ mouth
8. /juːs/ use

### Ex 2.3
1. worth
2. tank
3. death
4. thin
5. thread
6. thing
7. debt

## Task 4
### Ex 4.2
1. … another thing to consider is …
2. … in theory …
3. … the truth is that …
4. … the growth rate …
5. … a further theme …
6. … they thought that …
7. … this method …
8. … beneath the surface …
9. … this therapy might be used to …
10. … youth culture …

## Task 5
### Ex 5.1
So <u>whose</u> responsibility is it to <u>ensure</u> that <u>children</u> eat <u>healthily</u>? <u>Well</u>, clearly <u>parents</u> have a role, but while children are at <u>school</u>, it's difficult to keep <u>track</u> of what they are <u>eating</u>, so <u>some</u> would suggest that <u>schools</u> need to <u>encourage</u> healthy eating, and that this should be <u>reflected</u> in the <u>menus</u> they offer. Then there's the <u>food</u> industry. They've been <u>criticized</u> in the past for <u>high</u> levels of <u>sugar</u>, <u>fat</u>, and <u>salt</u> in food <u>and</u> for not giving <u>clear</u> information on the <u>levels</u> of different <u>ingredients</u> in food. And <u>finally</u> there's the <u>government</u>. Should <u>legislation</u> be used to <u>address</u> this <u>issue</u>?

## Ex 5.3

1. Well we know how this happened, <u>but do we know why it happened?</u>
2. Having looked at the effect of deforestation on the environment, <u>we will now discuss greenhouse gases and the roles they play</u>.
3. Most of our cotton is imported, <u>but we produce about 500,000 tonnes a year</u>.
4. The crime rate fell by 15 per cent last year, <u>but this year it's risen</u>.
5. The oil pump needs replacing, <u>not the filter</u>.

## Ex 5.5

As a <u>backdrop</u> <u>to</u> all of these activities, <u>particularly</u> after the Second World <u>War</u>, a lot of <u>effort</u> was put into <u>research</u> and development of <u>agriculture</u> in terms of <u>plant</u> breeding, breeding crops that were higher <u>yielding</u>, that were perhaps <u>disease</u>-resistant, and <u>so</u> on and so forth. <u>Also</u>, crops that might have better <u>quality</u>, better <u>bread-making</u> quality, higher <u>gluten</u> content, to make them <u>doughy</u>, higher <u>protein</u> content, and <u>so</u> on and so forth. <u>Research</u>, too, and this is <u>again</u> at one of the university <u>farms</u>, research into <u>livestock</u> production. <u>Understanding</u> how to better <u>manage</u> our livestock, <u>again</u> to make them <u>produce</u> more, <u>certainly</u>, but <u>also</u> to <u>produce</u> and influence the <u>quality</u> of the livestock <u>products</u>, whether that happens to be <u>milk</u> or <u>cheese</u>, come back to that in a <u>moment</u>, or indeed <u>meat</u>.

## Ex 5.7

Now to get to the <u>meat</u> of the lecture, the <u>basic</u> purpose of this <u>lecture</u> is to give you some <u>overview</u> of the <u>kind</u> of contemporary <u>academic</u> and <u>policy</u> debate about <u>globalization</u> and <u>particularly</u> about a very <u>specific</u>, although rather <u>general</u>, debate itself; <u>that</u> is, the <u>debate</u> on the <u>effect</u> of globalization on the <u>role</u> of the <u>state</u>. <u>So</u>, you see on the <u>overhead</u>, the <u>lecture's</u> going to be <u>kind</u> of in two <u>parts</u>: the <u>first</u> will be looking at <u>globalization</u>, <u>causes</u> and <u>consequences</u>, and more <u>particularly</u> a kind of <u>definition</u> of the <u>discussion</u> of some of the <u>competing</u> conceptions of <u>globalization</u>, that is, you know, <u>what</u> people say it <u>is</u>, so that we can then <u>discuss</u> in <u>some</u> detail, <u>hopefully</u>, this question of how globalization's affecting the <u>state</u>.

## Summary answers

### Ex 1

a. lose/loose, proof/prove, surge/search, three/free, very/ferry, seem/theme

## Ex 3

a. <u>Some</u> species of shark attack people, but <u>most</u> are harmless.
b. There <u>used</u> to be a Chemistry department, but it <u>closed</u> in 2006.
c. The aid provided to the victims was too <u>little</u>, too <u>late</u>.
d. Many banks <u>stopped</u> lending, when the government wanted them to lend <u>more</u>.

## Ex 4

a. and b. Students' own answers.
c. How is it helpful to study the phonemic symbols for different sounds?
   *If you learn the phonemic symbols, you will be able to check the pronunciation of any word in a learner's dictionary that includes phonemic transcriptions of words.*
d. Why is it helpful to be more aware of stressed words in a sentence?
   *Stressed words carry the new or important information of the utterance.*

## Unit 4

### Task 1

#### Ex 1.1

| /~ʒən/ | /~ʃən/ |
|---|---|
| decision | dimension |
| version | discussion |
| occasion | expression |
| conclusion | admission |
| supervision | expansion |
| confusion | |
| erosion | |

**Patterns:**

When the spelling is vowel sound + ~sion, the word is pronounced /~ʒən/.

When the spelling is ~nsion or ~ssion, the word is pronounced /~ʃən/.

#### Ex 1.2

| /~ʒə/ | /~ʃə/ | /~ʃɔː/ |
|---|---|---|
| measure | pressure | assure |
| leisure | | ensure |
| pleasure | | |
| exposure | | |
| closure | | |

**Patterns:**

When the spelling is vowel + ~sure, the word is pronounced /ʒə/.

When the spelling is ~nsure or ~ssure, the word is pronounced /~ʃə/.

## Task 3

### Ex 3.2

| | |
|---|---|
| 1. union | 8. username |
| 3. uniform | 9. usual |
| 6. unique | 10. uranium |
| 7. useful | |

### Ex 3.4

| | |
|---|---|
| 1. fʲuel | 6. fʲew |
| 2. vʲiew | 7. rescʲue |
| 3. argʲue | 8. distribʲute |
| 4. edʲucation | 9. assʲume |
| 5. cʲube | |

### Ex 4.2

| | |
|---|---|
| 1. /tʃɒp/ chop | 5. /ʃeə/ share |
| 2. /kætʃ/ catch | 6. /dɪtʃɪz/ ditches |
| 3. /ʃuːz/ shoes | 7. /tʃɪp/ chip |
| 4. /wɒtʃt/ watched | |

### Ex 4.3

| | |
|---|---|
| 1. chip | 4. share |
| 2. cash | 5. choose |
| 3. ditches | 6. washed |

### Ex 5.2

| | |
|---|---|
| 1. /sɜːtʃ/ search | 4. /tʃʌnk/ chunk |
| 2. /rɪdʒ/ ridge | 5. /bætʃ/ batch |
| 3. /eɪdʒ/ age | 6. /dʒiːp/ Jeep |

### Ex 5.3

| | |
|---|---|
| 1. rich | 4. ridge |
| 2. batch | 5. junk |
| 3. chunk | 6. surge |

## Task 6

### Ex 6.1

| Oo | oO |
|---|---|
| question | provide |
| problem | receive |
| recent | assist |
| reason | include |
| private | suggest |
| system | reduce |
| modern | prepare |
| certain | appear |
| factor | observe |

### Ex 6.2

1. 'export; ex'port
2. 'increase; in'crease
3. 'record; re'cord
4. 'present; pre'sent

### Ex 6.3

Rules for word stress in two-syllable words:

Most two-syllable <u>nouns</u> and <u>adjectives</u> have stress on the first syllable.

Most two-syllable <u>verbs</u> have stress on the second syllable.

## Summary answers

### Ex 1

| /ʃ/ | /tʃ/ | /dʒ/ |
|---|---|---|
| innovation | choices | suggest |
| distribution | watched | average |

| /ʒ/ | /s/ |
|---|---|
| confusion | system |
| unusual | service |

### Ex 2

/v/ innovation, average, service

/j/ confusion, distribution, unusual

### Ex 3

a. The 'contracts were signed last week.
   The metal con'tracts as it cools down.
b. It caused a lot of 'damage.
   How does it 'damage your health?
c. Why did they ob'ject to the proposal?
   Archaeologists are not sure what this 'object was used for.
d. What is the main 'focus of your research?
   We need to 'focus on the real issues.

## Unit 5

### Task 7
**Ex 1.1**

| /aɪ/ | /ɪ/ |
|------|-----|
| time | sit |
| site | think |
| life | bit |
| buy | win |
| write | |
| while | |
| might | |
| sign | |
| high | |
| like | |
| try | |

**Ex 1.3**
1. /lɪv/ (verb)
2. /laɪv/ (adverb, and also adjective)

**Ex 1.4**
1. /wɪl/ will /waɪl/ while
2. /fɪt/ fit /faɪt/ fight
3. /stɪl/ still /staɪl/ style
4. /hɪt/ hit /haɪt/ height
5. /lɪtə/ litter /laɪtə/ lighter
6. /hɪd/ hid /haɪd/ hide

**Ex 1.5**
1. Try the other side.
2. The height's fine.
3. This type of plant needs a lot of light.
4. There was a slight rise in the share value.

### Task 2
**Ex 2.1**

| /əʊ/ | /ɒ/ |
|------|-----|
| flow | cost |
| coast | rod |
| hope | not |
| show | lot |
| code | |
| cold | |
| road | |
| grow | |
| note | |
| load | |
| fold | |

**Ex 2.3**
**a. and b.**
1. /kɒst/ cost /kəʊst/ coast
2. /nɒt/ not /nəʊt/ note
3. /rɒd/ rod /rəʊd/ road
4. /sɒk/ sock /səʊk/ soak
5. /wɒnt/ want /wəʊnt/ won't
6. /fɒnd/ fond /fəʊnd/ phoned

**Ex 2.4**
1. Most of the gold is exported.
2. The hole in the ozone layer is growing.
3. Gross profits were down.
4. Can you cope with the workload?

### Task 3
**Ex 3.1**

| /eɪ/ | /æ/ | /ɑː/ |
|------|-----|------|
| plane | plan | heart |
| play | bad | dark |
| weigh | lack | part |
| face | | large |
| gain | | |
| make | | |
| scale | | |
| claim | | |

**Ex 3.3**
1. /læk/ lack /leɪk/ lake
2. /tæp/ tap /teɪp/ tape
3. /plæn/ plan /pleɪn/ plane
4. /lætə/ latter /leɪtə/ later
5. /ɑːm/ arm /eɪm/ aim
6. /mɑːk/ mark /meɪk/ make
7. /pɑːs/ pass /peɪs/ pace
8. /kɑːm/ calm /keɪm/ came

**Ex 3.4**
1. Can you explain this heavy rainfall?
2. That's quite a claim to make.
3. The future remains uncertain.
4. The failure rate is quite high.

### Task 4
**Ex 4.4**

In this presentation‿I'm going to talk‿about homeownership‿in the UK. First‿I'm going to focus‿on changes‿in the patterns‿of home ownership in the last 20 years, and provide‿an explanation for these changes. Then‿I'm going to describe the process‿of buying or selling‿a house. Finally_I'm going to_try to make some predictions_about the housing market.

## Ex 4.9

1. try /ʲ/ out
2. agree /ʲ/ on this
3. two /ʷ/ of them
4. driver /r/ error
5. radio /ʷ/ operator
6. media /r/ event
7. high /ʲ/ above the /ʲ/ Earth
8. How does this tie /ʲ/ in?

## Summary answers

### Ex 1

a. I think I'd like to carry on with life sciences, but I'm also interested in psychology. /aɪ/
b. I want to go into social work, so I'm studying sociology. /əʊ/
c. He came to Cardiff to give a paper on International relations. /eɪ/

### Ex 2

a. I_think_I'd like to_carry_/ʲ/_on with life sciences, but_I'm_also_/ʷ/_interested_ in_psychology.
b. I_wan(t)_to_ go_/ʷ/_into_social work, so_/ʷ/_ I'm studying sociology.
c. He_came to Cardiff to_give_a paper_ /r/_on_international relations.

### Ex 3

a. carry on – /ʲ/
b. go into – /ʷ/
c. paper on – /r/

### Ex 5

Note: Current thinking in language teaching methodology generally agrees with these statements, particularly with statement b.

a. Learners may sometimes be misunderstood if they confuse vowel and diphthong sounds, but the meaning is usually clear from the context.
b. Learners will generally still be perfectly intelligible if they don't link words as native speakers do.

## Unit 6

### Task 1
#### Ex 1.2

| | | | |
|---|---|---|---|
| 1. | flame | 6. | drum |
| 2. | gradual | 7. | traced |
| 3. | track; growth | 8. | blank |
| 4. | precise | 9. | fresh |
| 5. | plate | 10. | thread |

#### Ex 1.5

| | | | |
|---|---|---|---|
| 1. | scans | 6. | splashed |
| 2. | scarce | 7. | strange |
| 3. | species | 8. | slice |
| 4. | slow | 9. | stable |
| 5. | strategy | 10. | stone |

### Task 2
#### Ex 2.2

| | | | |
|---|---|---|---|
| 1. | distributed | 6. | extracted |
| 2. | explicit | 7. | abstract |
| 3. | transport | 8. | exploit |
| 4. | conflicts | 9. | comprises |
| 5. | unclear | 10. | extreme |

### Task 3
#### Ex 3.1

1. he
2. her
3. his

#### Ex 3.2

1. they've (they have); it's (it is)
2. that's (that is); it's (it is)
3. it'd (it would)
4. they're (they are)
5. can't (cannot); it's (it is); might've (might have)
6. I'd (I had)
7. to've (to have)
8. shouldn't've (should not have)

#### Ex 3.3

1. Vegetables are grown on about 60 per cent of farms in the area.
2. Perhaps he's left.
3. Which category does it fit in?
4. She's studying medicine.
5. I'll phone her secretary.

## Ex 3.4

1. It reacts with sulphur.
2. They'll send back the results on Tuesday.
3. It must be checked.
4. The low election turnout reflects growing apathy towards politics.
5. The engine tends to overheat in particular circumstances.

## Task 4

### Ex 4.1

1. good points
2. in Britain's
3. open prison
4. common ground

## Task 5

### Ex 5.2

As a backdrop to all of these activities, // particularly after the Second World War, // a lot of effort // was put into research and development of agriculture // in terms of plant breeding, // breeding crops that were higher yielding, // that were perhaps disease-resistant, // and so on and so forth. // Also, // crops that might have better quality, // better bread-making quality //, higher gluten content to make them doughy //, higher protein content, // and so on and so forth. // Research, too, // and this is again at one of the university farms, // research into livestock production. // Understanding how to better manage our livestock, // again to make them produce more, // certainly //, but also // to produce and influence the quality of the livestock products, // whether that happens to be milk // or cheese, // come back to that in a moment, // or indeed meat.

### Ex 5.3

Now to get to the meat of the lecture, // the basic purpose of this lecture // is to give you some overview // of the kind of contemporary academic // and policy debate about globalization // and particularly // about a very specific, // although rather general, debate itself; // that is, the debate on the effect of globalization on the role of the state. // So // you see on the overhead // the lecture's going to be kind of // in two parts: // the first will be looking at globalization, // causes and consequences // and more particularly // a kind of definition of the discussion // of some of the competing conceptions of globalization, // that is, // you know, what people say it is, // so that we can then discuss // in some detail hopefully //

this question of how globalization's // affecting the state.

## Summary answers

### Ex 2/3

a. 'spray' is the odd one out (It has the consonant cluster /spr/. The other words have the cluster /sp/.)

b. 'quarter' is the odd one out (It has no consonant cluster. The other words have the cluster /tr/.)

c. 'share' is the odd one out (It has the consonant sound /ʃ/. The other words have the cluster /sk/.)

d. 'store' is the odd one out (It has the consonant cluster/st/. The other words have the cluster /str/.)

e. 'construct' is the odd one out (It has four consonants, n + the cluster /str/. The other words have m + /pl/.)

f. 'inspect' is the odd one out (It has the cluster /sp/. The other words have the cluster /str/.)

### Ex 4

a. *You have got some interesting ideas // and make some good points, // but you could have developed these a bit more. // You must make sure // that you check your essay for spelling mistakes // and check the grammar is correct. // Perhaps // you should have asked your tutor to read through your work, // as he would have helped you improve it.*

## Unit 7

## Task 1

### Ex 1.1

| /eə/ | /ɪə/ |
|------|------|
| share | mere |
| where | appear |
| fair | severe |
| aware | near |
| square | adhere |
| wear | sphere |
| pair | year |
| chair | |
| bear | |
| there | |
| fare | |

## Ex 1.3

| | |
|---|---|
| 1. aware | 5. repair |
| 2. severe | 6. square |
| 3. mere | 7. adhere |
| 4. prepare | 8. bear; sphere |

## Task 2

### Ex 2.1

| /aʊ/ | /əʊ/ |
|---|---|
| allow | know |
| crowd | below |
| brown | follow |
| power | own |
| crown | slow |
| now | flow |
| shower | show |
| down | owe |
| powder | growth |

### Ex 2.2

| | |
|---|---|
| loud | south |
| doubt | amount |
| group | colour |
| account | course |
| court | enough |
| serious | young |
| sound | hour |
| various | ground |
| trouble | flavour |

### Ex 2.3

| | |
|---|---|
| 1. account | 6. allow |
| 2. power | 7. growth |
| 3. flow | 8. crowd |
| 4. powder | 9. amount |
| 5. doubt; serious | 10. flavour |

## Task 3

### Ex 3.2

| | |
|---|---|
| 1. choice | 5. destroyed |
| 2. voice | 6. exploit |
| 3. loyal | 7. voyages |
| 4. appointed | 8. joint; oil |

## Task 4

### Ex 4.1/4.2

I'm going to tell you something about the education system // before students get to the higher level. // There are several reasons for this. // One is, of course, // it's part of the plan of your course designers // to give you the experience of lectures // before you go into your real departments // in September or October, // but another reason // is that we have found in the past // that many students come to Britain // and they live and study here for a year or two // and they go away // without knowing some of the most basic facts // about the education system here.

It's <u>also true</u> // that the education system here, // <u>perhaps as in</u> your countries, // is changing very rapidly // and this means <u>that if you ask older</u> people // who don't <u>actually</u> have direct experience, // they probably give you information about the education system // <u>as it used to be</u>, // rather than as it actually is now.

Now // what qualifications, <u>as it were</u>, // do I have to speak on this particular subject? // Well I'm, // <u>as was said</u> in the introduction, // I'm here at Reading University // and my main <u>task</u> // is to look after international students here, like you //, who need academic language support. // Now between 20 and 23 per cent of the students in this university, // in Reading University, // do not have English as their first language // and did not receive their previous education in the United Kingdom. // So that's a large number of students, // <u>that's, you know</u> almost two and half thousand students, // in this university // were not actually educated in the United Kingdom // before they came to university // so you are amongst many. // <u>You are</u> // <u>you know</u> a minority // but you're a very large minority.

### Ex 4.3/4.4

1. We're going to <u>start</u> // by explaining <u>why</u> // we need a financial <u>market</u> at all.

2. What is the <u>role</u> // that is <u>played</u> by a financial <u>market</u>?

3. What is the <u>rationale</u> // for <u>having</u> a financial <u>market</u>?

4. And <u>then</u> // we're going to <u>move</u> on // and <u>explain</u> some of the <u>instruments</u> // that are <u>traded</u> in those <u>markets</u>.

5. I'm going to focus <u>mainly</u> // on the <u>stocks</u>, <u>bonds</u>, <u>bills</u>, // since these are by <u>far</u> the <u>easiest</u> to understand.